RIDEAU

RIDEAU

TEXT BY LARRY TURNER • PHOTOGRAPHY BY JOHN DE VISSER

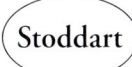
Stoddart

A BOSTON MILLS PRESS BOOK

CANADIAN CATALOGUING IN PUBLICATION DATA

Turner, Larry
  Rideau

Includes bibliographical references
ISBN 1-55046-136-2

1. Rideau Canal (Ont.) – History. 2. Rideau Canal (Ont.) – History – Pictorial works. I. De Visser, John, 1930– . II. Title.

HE401.R5T8 1995   386'.5'097137   C95-930572-6

© 1995, Larry Turner and John de Visser

First published in 1995 by
Stoddart Publishing Co. Limited
34 Lesmill Road
Toronto, Ontario
M3B 2T6
(416) 445-3333

A BOSTON MILLS PRESS BOOK
The Boston Mills Press
132 Main Street
Erin, Ontario
N0B 1T0

Design by Gillian Stead
Printed in Canada

OVERLEAF: *The village of Westport is nestled beneath the imposing Foley Mountain, where the Spy Rock lookout provides an outstanding view.*
FIRST PAGE: *Rugged shores dotted with cottages define island-studded Big Rideau Lake.*

The publisher gratefully acknowledges the support of the Canada Council,
Ministry of Culture, Tourism and Recreation, Ontario Arts Council and
Ontario Publishing Centre in the development of writing and publishing in Canada.

Stoddart books are available for bulk purchase for sales promotions, premiums, fundraising, and seminars.
For details contact:

Special Sales Department, Stoddart Publishing Co. Limited
34 Lesmill Road, Toronto, Ontario M3B 2T6
Tel. 1-416-445-3333   Fax 1-416-445-5967

CONTENTS

A century of fishing for lake trout, bass and pike at Fancy Free cottage on Big Rideau Lake.

Acknowledgments	7	11.	Rideau Lakes Cottages	75
1. Through a Land of Contrasts	9	12.	Polished Mahogany and Gleaming Brass	81
2. Patterns of Settlement	21	13.	Perth on the Tay	85
3. Lieutenant-Colonel John By of the Royal Engineers	27	14.	Smiths Falls and the Swale	91
4. The Royal Sappers and Miners	33	15.	Merrickville, Burritt's Rapids and the Long Reach	99
5. The Lockmaster	37	16.	King of the Rideau	107
6. Kingston: To Preserve and Defend	45	17.	Through the Heart of the Nation's Capital	111
7. The Jones Falls Dam	53	Map		116
8. Bedford Mills	57	A Note on Sources		118
9. The Drowned Lands	63	Select Bibliography		119
10. Don Warren: Defender of the Rideau	71			

The thundering falls at Hogsback. Ottawa area pioneer Bradish Billings, his wife, Lamira Dow, and their baby daughter, Sabra, miraculously escaped an accidental descent of the falls in a canoe in 1814.

ACKNOWLEDGMENTS

John de Visser and Larry Turner are grateful to many people who contributed time, advice and water transport during the process of creating this book. Special thanks go to Robert Sneyd, with whom we toured Big Rideau Lake on *Gran D*, and Sarah and Murray Gould in *Warpath* as well as Cameron and Jamie Graham in *L'Aventure*, both on the Long Reach. Don Warren guided us around Lake Opinicon, Judy and Barry Blann of Melody Lodge Marina provided a boat on Cranberry Lake, and Ed Bartholomew chauffered us in the purple boat. We appreciate the contribution made by Jim Ives of Murphy's Point Provincial Park; Frank Phelan of the Queen's University Biological Station; John Bonser, Judy Sutherland, Lindsay Penney and lock staff of the Rideau Canal; Arthur Briggs-Jude; Harold Nichol; Linda and Jimmy Potter; Tom and Pamela Gough and Allan and Ruth Burger of Fancy Free Island; Phil and Fran Turner; the Manotick Classic Boat Club; Mills Mooney and family of Drop Anchor Island; and many other people who may appear in these photographs or who made arrangements for photographs to be taken. Many thanks to editors Kathy Fraser and Noel Hudson, designer Gillian Stead, and John Denison at Boston Mills Press.

Rideau lakelands. The Rideau Canal linked two rivers and a series of lakes.

1

THROUGH A LAND OF CONTRASTS

The Rideau Canal stretches across Eastern Ontario by way of river, lake, channel, and masonry locks, winding through farm, forest, village and urban landscapes. A masterpiece of engineering design, the canal emerged from the wilderness between the years 1826 and 1832 under the direction of Lieutenant-Colonel John By and the Royal Engineers. It is North America's oldest continuously operating canal and links Ottawa, Canada's national capital, with the historic city of Kingston on Lake Ontario was named a National Historic Site in 1967. Since 1972 the Rideau Canal has operated as a Heritage Canal, managed by Parks Canada, now within the Ministry of Canadian Heritage.

In 1832 the rivers and lakes of the waterway were connected by 18 miles (29 km) of excavated canal channels and twenty-three lock stations with forty-seven locks. "Canal," as used here, means both the narrow navigable channel and the entire waterway, which encompasses not only the shoreline of lake and river, but also the watershed of two major river systems flowing in opposite directions. Upper Rideau Lake forms the headwaters from where the Cataraqui River flows south and west to Lake Ontario and the Rideau River flows north and east to the Ottawa River. Beginning at chapter 6, this book follows the course of the waterway, moving north from Kingston to Ottawa.

The canal still uses many original or slightly modified operating mechanisms, reflecting both innovation and tradition in canal construction and technology and contemporary preservation. The architectural heritage left behind by the stonemasons who constructed the canal and the patterns of settlement created by the waterway do much to define the Rideau region. As the canal shifts from natural to rural to urban landscapes, it passes through places marked by the effects of history and patterns of land use.

Unlike such lakeland regions as Muskoka and the Kawarthas, which are relatively homogenous in nature, the Rideau region is known for its diversity. There is diversity in economic regions, land use, settlement patterns, landforms and character. The Rideau watershed stretches for dozens of miles on both sides of the canal in drainage systems, through creeks, lakes and tributaries. As an economic corridor, the Rideau anchored settlement patterns and lured industries deep into lands beyond the watershed. As a canal, the Rideau Waterway

The lock station at Upper Brewers. While most Rideau Canal lock stations became centres of growth, where bridges and communities sprang up, many, like Upper Brewers, have retained their rural charm.

was originally built to serve military intentions, but was transformed into a commercial and recreational transportation system, and that caused further direct changes in land use and settlement.

The Rideau Canal links a land of contrasts. The bedrock changes from a limestone base along the shores of Lake Ontario when it meets the Frontenac Axis, the southernmost intrusion of the rocky Canadian Shield, just east of Kingston. The Kingston limestone, which helped shape the architectural character of that Loyalist garrison town, meets the landscape of the Shield at the base of Cranberry Lake. North of there, the Rideau Canal takes on the same rugged character of the lakelands and broad preCambrian foundation of Northern Ontario, Québec, Manitoba and Saskatchewan for approximately 45 miles (77 km), until the area around Rideau Ferry marks the transition back to the limestone plain that underlays the lower Ottawa River Valley. This sedimentary bedrock, part of an ancient sea, changes the nature of the landscape. Where it is layered with silt beds and clay plains, the fertility of the soil increases, but where it is poorly drained, the land is marginal and resistant to agricultural settlement.

The interaction between humans and their natural environment creates a cultural landscape. Canal construction and the management of water totally altered the nature of the Cataraqui and Rideau Rivers by linking the two systems, creating several new lakes, widening existing lakes, and taming unnavigable rapids and waterfalls. Lieutenant-Colonel John By designed a slackwater canal system in which high dams raised the water level to flood the rapids and back up the water to a navigable depth. Each stillwater so created would stretch upriver to the base of the dam at the next set of rapids. In *Building the Rideau Canal: A Pictorial History*, historian Robert Passfield has identified this method of construction as unprecedented in its scope of engineering vision and scale of technological challenge. (Previously most canal cuts in England were made independent of rivers, and slackwater canals in the United States were small feeders to a larger system.) The widespread flooding altered natural environments and imposed a rigid system of water control that is maintained to the present day. The engineering achievements of the Rideau were considered among the technological wonders of the world, especially in light of the stubborn determination required to complete the canal in the middle of a thinly populated wilderness within a span of only six years.

Some pre-canal villages clustered around the mill sites of Kingston Mills, Brewers Mills, Chaffey's Mills, Perth, Merrickville, Burritt's Rapids and Kemptville, but most development resulted from the creation of the canal. Many construction workers chose to remain in the Rideau corridor, and once it was navigable, the waterway was also an important immigration gateway bringing settlers along its path into the region. Indeed, during the time when the Rideau Canal was the dominant Canadian

Straight lines on curved fields near Sunbury, a transition area where the underlying limestone plain and preCambrian Shield meet.

Turning over the slabs of cheddar at Forfar cheese factory, the last of its kind in Leeds, once one of the dominant cheese-making counties in Eastern Ontario, where forty-six factories were in operation in 1944.

pathway into the interior, between 1832 and 1847, it received a major infusion of Irish immigrants through the process of chain migration (communities formed in the new land based on kinship and neighbourhood in the old); several townships on the Rideau River such as Marlborough, Montague and Wolford still retained a population of over seventy percent Irish origin by 1900.

Lock stations were more than crossroads in the landscape; they were gateways to the canal for imports and exports. Lock, dam and weir sites along the Rideau accomodated grist mills to grind grain and sawmills to process wood. In the latter half of the nineteenth century, textile mills were developed at Burritt's Rapids, Merrickville, New Edinburgh (Ottawa), Perth and Smiths Falls; stove and agricultural implement factories started up at Merrickville and Smiths Falls, and cheese factories were established throughout Carleton, Frontenac, Leeds and Grenville, and Lanark Counties. The woollen mills are now nothing but ghostly reminders of an industrial past, but cheese factories survive at Forfar and Balderson.

The forest and bedrock helped shape the history of the Rideau corridor. In the early days along the Rideau many lumbering communities, from winter camboose shanties to mill-towns, were sustained by the square timber

A diminishing landscape on the Rideau Canal: the juxtaposition of canal and pastoral space. A cruiser drifts by a listless herd of cows between Upper and Lower Brewers Locks.

Three sections of the waterway are so long as to require bridges at some distance from lock stations in rural areas: at the Long Reach, between Big and Lower Rideau Lakes, and here, crossing Cranberry Lake at Brass Point Bridge.

trade, sawlog cutting and sawmilling. Up until the recent past, the forests of native white pine, oak, elm, hemlock, cedar, tamarack and maple were harvested for a seemingly endless demand for wood, for canal timber, local construction, railway ties, cordwood, furniture and carriage-making factories. Stands of maple continue to support an important maple sugar industry. The mining industry of the Rideau has all but disappeared, but from 1860 to the 1920s, shallow deposits of apatite (for fertilizer) and mica (for insulation and unbreakable glass) sustained a regionally important activity, especially in Bedford and North Burgess Townships. Deposits of iron ore, feldspar and graphite in the Frontenac Axis of the Canadian Shield also attracted prospectors. Quarries of limestone and sandstone were not only used for the masonry of the Rideau Canal, but also provided the material for some of the Rideau's finest architectural treasures.

The water-power potential and the bridges around lock and dam sites also attracted town development. The construction of lock stations and bridges at several locations helped ensure their future role as vital centres of the system. Even where villages did not develop, later recreational communities did, attracted by the seclusion as well as the accessibility of the countryside. The pattern of settlement on the Rideau was engraved before the arrival of the railways.

The Rideau Canal helped shape the city of Ottawa and continues to play a central role in the character of that city. But at its opposite end, the Rideau Canal emerged into Cataraqui Bay, some distance from the village of Barriefield and the city of Kingston. When the canal was completed, Kingston was already a half-century old, and the canal formed part of the mantle of defence and security surrounding this strategic city. Kingston's primary paths of trade and commerce focused on east-west transhipment between the St. Lawrence River and Lake Ontario, and south to the Erie Canal via Oswego, so the Rideau conveniently plugged into existing economies and provided a channel to resources in the hinterland. The Rideau Canal helped reinforce Kingston's role as an entranceway to the St. Lawrence, but it never influenced the city in the way it inspired Ottawa.

The Rideau Canal runs through Ottawa in a channel separate from the Rideau River. The Hogsback Falls and the dam and locks there mark the point of separation of the river and canal. The two waterways are very different in temperament. The river cascades majestically over the falls and then rushes through a broad valley before spilling over the escarpment at Rideau Falls into the Ottawa River at New Edinburgh, just below Ottawa City Hall. The industries at the Rideau Falls were once shining examples of the boisterous milling tradition of the Ottawa Valley.

The river whitewater is fierce in comparison with the unhurried passage of the canal backwater. The canal in Ottawa flows listlessly

Hartwell's Locks, a scene of pastoral splendor wedged between the campus of Ottawa's Carleton University and the Experimental Farm.

Lockmen are busy at Ottawa's Hogsback Locks. St. John the Baptist Ukrainian Catholic Church is seen in the distance.

through Hogsback Locks and through a channel toward the rural charm of Hartwell's Locks, wedged between the campus of Carleton University to the east and the Experimental Farm to the west. At Dows Lake, the canal opens up into a placid pond that is a lure for recreational boaters. The Deep Cut then drains the canal slowly through residential areas into the heart of the city. Bordered by the Queen Elizabeth and Colonel By Drive and arched over by several historic and other more recent bridges, including the elegant 1913-14 Bank Street Bridge, this section of the canal was the first to benefit from landscaping efforts by the Ottawa Improvement Commission at the turn of the century. The cement walls have given the canal a harder edge, but the gardens, parks and walkways make the waterway a favourite destination for pedestrians and bicyclists, especially during the tulip festival. The canal glides past Frank Clair Stadium, the Aberdeen Pavilion, rows of stately Victorian homes, the University of Ottawa, the National Arts Centre, the Confederation Conference Centre (old Union Station), and then meets the Ottawa flight of locks. The eight masonry locks that fall between Parliament Hill and the Château Laurier, that section of the canal that is one of Canada's greatest and most recognizable landmarks, are stunning in their beauty and craftsmanship.

The contemporary canal cuts through working and recreational landscapes; broad, flat, limestone plains and rugged outcrops of undulating rock. The River Styx, High Rock

The elegant Bank Street Bridge, built in 1913–14.

Dunder, Jones Falls, Foley Mountain, the Rocky Narrows, Smiths Falls Swale, the Marlborough Forest, Long Reach, and the Deep Cut all belong to the same corridor but vary greatly in appearance and form. The only landscape feature that recurs throughout the system is the lock station. But even the stations take on the character of their immediate environment; the busy crossroad stations at Smiths Falls can be contrasted with the isolated and pristine Davis Lock.

Urban expansion, hardening shorelines, disappearing wetlands, diminishing water quality, and recreational overuse are real threats to the vitality of the Rideau Waterway. Sustainable solutions are being discussed by public interest groups, canal users, residents and government bodies. The survival of this navigable waterway as one of Canada's most significant transportation systems and heritage waterways is so far the result of the patience, operational skill and the preservationist philosophy of those who manage and use it. Plans are in place to help preserve the features of the cultural landscape and the character of the waterway. However, it will be the users and the residents who ultimately shape the future of the canal. The Rideau Canal has been a constant since 1832, but its construction precipitated an evolutionary process that continues today. The challenge is to sustain the character of the canal while responding to the changes of the future.

The Rideau Canal in the heart of Ottawa descends to the Ottawa River, framed by the Gothic-inspired buildings of Parliament Hill and the Château Laurier, one of Canada's original grand railway hotels.

The Lally family emigrated from Ireland in the 1840s, and they built this, their second homestead in the 1880s in North Burgess Township, within present-day Murphy's Point Provincial Park. As is typical of many marginal farms planted on the bedrock of the Canadian Shield, a young forest now emerges here, on fields that were once cleared with back-breaking labour.

2

PATTERNS OF SETTLEMENT

The chain of lakes and rivers north of the St. Lawrence River were known to have potential for settlement from the time of the earliest surveys. The Rideau and Cataraqui Rivers were not, however, part of the mainstream of the developing frontiers of Upper Canada until the Rideau Canal created a way into the interior after 1832. Before construction of the canal, limited settlement was encouraged by the existence of mill sites at rapids, individual settlement leaders, an imposed military settlement and assisted emigration. After construction of the canal was complete, immigrants no longer had to be pushed or pulled along its path.

Sir Frederick Haldimand, governor of Québec, sent an exploring party to the Rideau corridor in 1783 to search for viable lands on which to settle Loyalist refugees from the American War of Independence. Lieutenant Gershom French of Jessup's Loyal Rangers reported lands "good on both sides [of] the River," but the St. Lawrence River and eastern Lake Ontario received most of the United Empire Loyalists after 1784. Except for the original Kingston mills built under government supervision by Robert Clark and David Brass in 1783–84, the Rideau and Cataraqui Rivers remained empty of European settlement until the 1790s.

In 1790 Roger Stevens, a Loyalist who had last served in James Roger's King's Rangers, applied for a mill site on the Rideau River. The site was acquired by William Merrick shortly before Stevens's death by drowning in 1793. The village of Merrickville grew from this original cluster of mills in much the same way as Burritt's Rapids downstream, named after Stevens's son-in-law, Stephen Burritt, and his family. Burritt's Rapids developed into a local agricultural service centre and milling site, and Merrickville eventually emerged as a nineteenth-century industrial powerhouse on the Rideau Canal.

Upper Canada's first lieutenant-governor, John Graves Simcoe, encouraged free grants and settlement schemes, especially among Americans whom he thought would gladly take advantage of the opportunity to be once more under benevolent British rule. Roger Stevens's brother, Abel Stevens, petitioned to bring American Baptists from Vermont to Kitley and Bastard Townships in 1793, and by 1795, fifty-two families had settled. Similar proprietary schemes undertaken by Samuel Stafford and Joseph Easton in Montague and

Lilacs clustered alone in a field often signal the former location of a home. In this case, the Jesse Chester House in Montague Township is still intact on Highway 43 between Smiths Falls and Merrickville, and dates from the construction period of the Rideau Canal.

In Lanark County, where dairy farming dominates, cows assume rights on County Road 10.

Wolford Townships created what was known as the Rideau Settlement, but by 1796, these and other townships returned to normal patterns of land granting to avoid speculation. However, the Rideau area still lacked pull until the government decided that a strategic defence and settlement scheme was necessary after the War of 1812.

The Rideau military settlement was part of an ambitious strategy to reinforce defences, a plan by government to fill the corridor between Kingston and the Ottawa River with discharged soldiers and assisted immigrants after the war between the British in Canada and the Americans. The war had exposed the weakness of using the St. Lawrence River as a lifeline to the colony of Upper Canada, and the British military saw the Rideau corridor as an alternative supply line. A loyal population along the proposed canal route was essential.

It is ironic that, owing to the overgenerous provision of free land-grants to the United Empire Loyalists after 1784, sections of the Rideau corridor had become what historian Glenn J. Lockwood has described as an empty frontier, where absentee owners waited for development to come to them rather than initiating it themselves. Indeed, the military settlement had to be located northwest of the Rideau Lakes on land not already claimed. Thus the first settlement depot was located in 1816 at a site on the Tay River about 9 miles (15 km) distant from the proposed canal. Perth developed more as a cul-de-sac than as a strategic garrison. A depot was also established in 1818 at Richmond on the Jock River, the second-largest tributary of the Rideau River after the Tay, and another in 1820 at Lanark.

The military settlers were mostly decommissioned officers and regulars from British and colonial units that fought against Napoleon in Europe and against Americans on the frontiers of Lower and Upper Canada. They were a varied assortment of men and came from naval, cavalry, artillery, militia and fencible units in England, Ireland, Scotland, Wales and Newfoundland, as well as two Swiss regiments, de Watteville and de Meuron. Military settlers accompanied by families or officers supported by half-pay pensions were likely to take up their lands, but single men and soldiers frequently drifted away from the inland territory when other, greener pastures were still available.

The military settlement dovetailed nicely with an assisted immigration scheme also designed to help populate Upper Canada's interior with loyal subjects. Although the plan later became a method of settling families displaced by the Highland Clearances and unemployment in the Scottish textile industries, the immigration helped augment the civilian nature of the settlement. The military settlement and subsequent patterns of Irish-Protestant immigration transformed the character of emerging communities by infusing settlers of British backgrounds into a region originally more American in nature.

The two-hundredth anniversary of South Burgess and Bastard Townships, south of Big Rideau Lake, revived nineteenth-century costume for these youngsters at a special parade in 1994 in Portland.

The Rideau Canal vitalized inland settlement. French-Canadian, and Irish labourers, Scottish stonemasons and others were attracted by the opportunities of canal construction. Immigrants who entered Upper Canada between 1832 and 1847 mostly came by way of the Rideau Canal, and many found the waterway an attractive place to settle. The military character of the system was soon displaced by the commercial viability of the canal, and by the 1850s, civilian administration took over its operation. Before Confederation, the lumber empire of the Rideau was largely confined to the rugged lands of the Canadian Shield, where sawmills thrived on the Tay River and at Hogg's Bay, Westport, Bedford Mills, Morton, Brewers Mills and Kingston Mills. By the 1880s there were more than forty-five industries using Rideau River water power: clusters of grist, saw and textile mills at Port Elmsley, Andrewsville, Burritt's Rapids, Manotick, and especially at Smiths Falls, Merrickville and New Edinburgh. Mills and farms attracted workers and immigrants, but by 1900, many were tempted away from Eastern Ontario to more modern and centralized industries in cities and by the agricultural potential of the American and Canadian West.

The Rideau Waterway receded in economic importance just at the time when a new generation of urban-dwellers was seeking opportunities for natural and spiritual revival away from the pressures of the crowded city. Increased affluence and leisure time and improved modes of transportation opened up the Rideau Waterway to a new class of seasonal and temporary residents—campers, cottage owners and tourists. The recreational development of the shores and islands of the Rideau Canal helped balance rural and village depopulation until after the Second World War, when the growth of satellite communities and suburbs of Ottawa greatly increased population pressure on the Rideau River section of the system.

The Rideau Waterway landscape today balances large tracts of forests with marginal as well as productive farms, manufacturing areas, residential communities in cities, towns and villages, and recreational communities along the river and the lakes. Layers of change and patterns of survival make up the quilted pattern of land use on the waterway.

A statue of Lieutenant-Colonel John By, the founder of Bytown (Ottawa) and the builder of the Rideau Canal, near his original home in Major's Hill Park across from Parliament Hill.

3

LIEUTENANT-COLONEL JOHN BY OF THE ROYAL ENGINEERS

When Lieutenant-Colonel John By began planning and designing the Rideau Canal in 1826, the land between Kingston and Bytown was a wilderness, with only a handful of tiny communities on the Cataraqui and Rideau Rivers, and clusters of settlement below and above the chain of Rideau Lakes. Rugged roads crept north from Gananoque, Brockville, Maitland and Prescott, and west from Bytown to Richmond. The rivers were wild passages of whitewater and swifts, fed by the streams, creeks, broad pools and lakes that formed the headwaters. John By was one of an early generation of engineers who thought it possible to transform whole landscapes to serve the purposes of humankind.

Born in 1779 near Lambeth Palace in London, England, By attended the Royal Military Academy at Woolwich and was commissioned in the Royal Artillery before embarking on a career as a Royal Engineer. The engineers and the artillery were both military corps under the direction of the British Ordnance Department, whose master-general sat in the Cabinet. Ordnance was called upon for advice and expertise in military, civilian and colonial affairs, and John By was posted to Québec City on two different tours of duty to work on canal projects and fortifications. He served under the Duke of Wellington in the Peninsular War and supervised Ordnance facilities in England after 1812. After his first wife died in 1814, By married Esther March in 1818. His new wife was an heiress, and she enabled By to enjoy a temporary respite at the family estate, Shernfold Park, in Frant, Sussex, until the time of his assignment to build the Rideau Canal in 1826.

Contemporary British engineers had learned that they had the power to shape the landscape. Lieutenant-Colonel John By was given permission to do just that in one of the far colonies of the Empire. Facing massive physical obstacles, and lacking frequent, or even knowledgeable, contact with his superiors, By had to design, plan and create construction specifications and drawings for a system to transform a wild river to tame channel, and all within a limited time-span, using outside contractors.

It was one of the largest projects ever undertaken by the Royal Engineers up to that time. The extensive use of contractors was unprecedented. Several of the engineering structures, including the Jones Falls Dam, were among the largest and most complex of the time. Decisions had to be made in the middle of the project, while construction was ongoing, that would completely alter the way the canal was used. Decisions made in 1828, resulting from By's foresight in making the locks and channel large enough to handle steamboats and general commerce, and his radical concept of turning the Rideau–Cataraqui system into a slackwater canal instead of one with extensive excavation, had an irreversible impact on the nature of the system.

The first design alteration allowed the canal to develop a commercial orientation beyond its original military purpose. Instead of a canal limited to standard gunboats and other small canal craft, it was built to handle the steamboats that were then changing the nature of inland navigation. By had argued for locks 50 feet (15 m) wide instead of the specified 25 feet (8 m) recommended by government. A compromise was reached, so that Rideau locks were constructed 33 feet (10 m) wide and 134 feet (41 m) long, with a draft of 5 1/2 feet (1.7 m).

The second decision, to use a slackwater system, turned the former turbulent rivers into vast navigable stretches of lake and river, flooding depths for navigation back from one dam and lock station to the next. It meant that Rideau dams were designed to hold back water and were supplied with waste weirs. The slackwater design could be used on the Rideau Canal because the natural riverbanks were high enough to retain the raised water with minimal embankment and the areas that had to be flooded were low-lying rock or wetlands and of minimal value. Unlike the early Erie and Welland Canals with their towpaths, the Rideau navigation required self-propulsion by oar, sail, or steam engine.

Part of the reason the canal survived commercial decline was because it had become an essential water-control system for the entire Rideau corridor.

Lieutenant-Colonel By had to manage several contractors who were working simultaneously along the system with minimal supervision. At some locations, contractors had neither the skills nor the perseverance to complete what they started. The failure of structures at places such as Long Island and Hogsback taxed the resolve and ingenuity of engineers. A single breach in a dam, one impossible situation, could interrupt progress or even doom the entire system to total failure. One can imagine By's fear and frustration when the Hogsback Dam failed twice before engineers succeeded in designing a structure that could withstand the torrent. In his report on the second failure of the Hogsback Dam in the spring of 1829, By related how he had just told a worker "You see what perseverance will do, the dam is saved," when suddenly, "I felt it tremble, and instantly ordered the men to run. I stood and looked at it for a few seconds, when the stones fell from under my feet as I ran off."

The Rideau Canal was built with stone, wood and iron. Many of the original cast- and wrought-iron pieces were designed by Royal Engineers and shaped or installed by blacksmiths on-site. Rideau lock gates were originally framed from local stands of oak, but since the 1890s, the dimension timber is Pacific-coast Douglas fir, now chemically treated to withstand the elements.

The work force was made up of Irish immigrants and French Canadians, some of them labourers with experience at other major projects such as the Welland and Oswego canals. Artisans from all over the British Isles, including stonemasons from Scotland, were brought to the site. The work sites themselves and a transient, potentially volatile workforce were difficult to control by contractors and engineers. The 7th and 15th Companies of Royal Sappers and Miners were required to guard stores, keep order at construction sites and provide skills where necessary. Working conditions were wretched, and many workers and their employers succumbed to malaria and other hazards of the workplace, including death by drowning, and accidents resulting from handling quantities of iron, stone and timber and the primitive use of dynamite in rock excavation.

Everyone underestimated the cost of the project at the beginning, but Lieutenant-

A gun port in the Kingston Mills blockhouse allows light to radiate into the interior. The blockhouse once housed lock staff and their families, and was meant to garrison soldiers in time of war. Lieutenant-Colonel John By wanted blockhouses at every lock station, but they were built only at those with strategic locations, such as the entrance locks from Kingston.

Colonel By had no idea how far the project would spiral out of control. Nor was By aware of the extent to which cost overruns would affect his stature as a Royal Engineer and would be misunderstood by the remote British Treasury. The creation of the Rideau Canal, accomplished within a time frame of six years (most of the canal was actually completed by 1831), in the face of obstacles and difficulties of design, construction and communication, was an engineering achievement of overwhelming significance. However, British Ordnance and Treasury officials had no idea of the scope of the project, nor of the increased costs caused by necessary changes to plans and problems experienced during construction. Their expectations were at one time based on a ridiculously low estimate of 169,000 pounds sterling, so that when costs rose to a final expenditure of 822,000 pounds, By was the one who took the blame.

In shaping the kind of canal he thought was possible and necessary for the region, rather than the canal envisaged by distant military officials and the Treasury, Lieutenant-Colonel By harmed his own position. By was vindicated by officials who were familiar with the canal, but he was dealt with harshly by the lords of the Treasury at home, who had no understanding of the magnitude of his achievement. Lieutenant-Colonel By was called home to explain his actions before two enquiries but was never actually called to testify. Although exonerated, he never felt that he had been vindicated, and requested from his Ordnance superiors in July 1833 that "I may be honored with some public distinction as will show that my character as a soldier is without stain, and that I have not lost the confidence or good opinion of my Government."

John By died prematurely in 1836, before he could receive the recognition of his peers that was eventually delivered in a letter to his widow, Esther. By is buried at Frant, where a memorial stone in the church and the graveyard extol his exemplary achievement. A statue of By overlooks the Ottawa Locks and Parliament Hill, near the site of his home in Major's Hill Park, and he will be remembered as the insightful, challenging and dynamic engineer who created one of the most outstanding examples of canal engineering in the world.

The canoe and the tug at Newboro Lock, formerly the workboats of ancient and more recent uses on inland waterways.

4

THE ROYAL SAPPERS AND MINERS

The Royal Sappers and Miners were special construction corps of the British Army originally formed in 1772. The 7th and 15th Companies were recruited largely in Scotland and England for work in the construction of the Rideau Canal. Commanded by officers of the Corps of Royal Engineers on the Rideau Canal, they were made up of stonecutters, masons, blacksmiths and carpenters experienced at foundation work, drainage systems, dams, bridges, weirs and locks. Among their numbers were Scots and Cornish miners and masons experienced in dry stone keywork, which was an important element of Rideau Canal masonry that made it capable of withstanding submerged conditions and long winters.

The Royal Engineers designed the canal, and civilian contractors built it, but the Royal Sappers and Miners were often appealed to for assistance when design and construction met with great difficulty, when contractors abandoned their work. They were also called out to guard stores and keep order at work sites. They served guard duty and as skilled labour at Long Island, Merrickville, the Narrows Lock, Jones Falls and Chaffey's Lock. However, they had the greatest impact in Bytown, where they cleared the entrance channel and erected government buildings; at Hogsback, where the dam proved a challenge; and at the Isthmus, later known as Newboro.

The contractor in charge of excavating the Isthmus between Newboro and Upper Rideau Lake ran into such difficulties that the work was abandoned, and then taken up in 1829 by two officers of the Royal Engineers, fifty-nine Sappers and Miners of the 7th Company and two hundred and fifty labourers. Lieutenant-Colonel By had planned that the channel at Newboro would be deep enough to create an uninterrupted stretch of water for 30 miles (50 km) between Chaffey's Lock and Poonamalie. The rock proved so resistant and the malaria-carrying mosquitoes so persistent that locks had to be installed at Newboro and the Narrows to avoid insects and extensive excavation.

John Mactaggart, clerk of works on the canal and author of *Three Years in Canada* (1829), describes the harrowing experience of surviving an attack of malaria. The symptoms "generally come on with an attack of bilious fever, dreadful vomiting, pains in the back and loins, general debility, loss of appetite.... After being in this state for eight or ten days, the yellow

The Merrickville blockhouse was designed to garrison the local militia and soldiers in time of war and to provide a shelter and home to the lockmaster and his family in peace. Since 1966 this National Historic Site has been managed by the Merrickville and District Historical Society as a museum.

jaundice is likely to ensue, and then fits of trembling.... For two or three hours before they arrive, we feel so cold that nothing will warm us...and then the shaking begins. Our very bones ache, teeth chatter, and the ribs are sore, continuing thus in great agony.... This over, we find the malady has run one of its rounds, and start out of the bed in a feeble state."

Primitive methods of rock excavation exacted a horrible toll on men inexperienced with explosives. Holes were driven by pounding a rock drill with a sledgehammer. Next, gunpowder and blasting powder were tamped down, and the men attracted by high wages for handling powder and lighting fuses then risked life and limb from flying stone and premature explosions.

Near the site of St. Mary's cemetery where many workers are buried was a little garrison with officer's quarters, stores, barracks, a guardhouse, magazine, hospital, shops, and several Sappers' and worker shanties. The site today shows no evidence of these early buildings, but on the opposite side of the cut, the village of Newboro dates from that time. At every construction site, workers lived in rude shelters under the control of contractors. Most of the workers had recently immigrated or were attracted to the project by the opportunity of making higher wages than they could ever hope to get in existing urban or rural areas. While working and living conditions and rates of pay seem abysmal by today's standards, the labourers were in a position to retain up to two-thirds of their pay while working on the canal.

Seventy-one members of the Royal Sappers and Miners were discharged in 1831, forty-one of whom received land and settled along the canal. Thirty-five had deserted, twenty-two died and thirty-one returned to Great Britain. Of those who stayed, several made up the first generation of lockmasters on the Rideau Canal, and all received land grants for their efforts. They were the most privileged of the huge work-force that helped build the canal. Many workers stayed in hopes of profiting from the prospects of the new waterway, but many moved on, and many more lie buried at forgotten cemeteries along the system. By John By's death in 1836, under the shadow of official censure for cost overruns in building the canal, he was linked with the many other workers who died in desperate circumstances, all without seeing the completion or triumph of their efforts.

The tranquillity of a Rideau lock station. A wooden swing-bridge at Lower Brewers Lock.

5

THE LOCKMASTER

A lockmaster on the Rideau Canal opens lock gates, regulates water flow, manages boat traffic, keeps records, collects lockage fees, supervises landscaping, and often swings bridges where they are located at locks. The lockmaster also serves as a tourist guide, expected to advise on weather forecasting, fishing hot spots, camping sites and local news. Like last century's postmaster, innkeeper and train-station agent, the lockmaster has wide-ranging responsibilities including being the best source of information around. The job looks simple, idyllic, even pastoral–but those long weekends!

Over time, the character and nature of those who have served as lockmaster has changed. The first batch of lockmasters were mostly military men discharged from the 7th and 15th Companies of the Royal Sappers and Miners who were offered the option, once the canal was completed, to settle on the Rideau instead of returning to Great Britain. Candidates for the position were expected to be able to read, write legibly, and understand simple arithmetic and accounting methods. The Royal Engineers also wanted lockmasters under the age of fifty, in good health, and of steady and sober moral character.

So that the new lockmasters would effectively represent the authority and prestige of the British Ordnance Department, they were issued uniforms that emphasized their position. The intent may have been to avoid the kind of feuds that arose between canallers and the "Yankee traders" known to serve as Erie Canal locktenders, or lock-keeps. Each Rideau lockmaster received a blue greatcoat with a scarlet collar and Ordnance buttons, as well as a blue cloth shell-jacket with a scarlet collar and cuffs and decorated with an embroidered crown on the right arm. Each also received grey cloth trousers and a blue forage cap with a scarlet band.

When the provincial board of works assumed management of the canal in 1856, civilian lockmasters were still expected to be hardworking, intelligent, good-tempered and sober. That was a difficult standard to maintain in the face of falling canal revenues, lockages and salaries and frequent intemperance. When the new federal government assumed control in 1868, responsibility for the canal was eventually given to the Department of Railways and Canals, where, between 1894 and 1934, Superintendent Arthur T. Phillips tried to revive the notion of a military facility.

The upper lock at Jones Falls, filled to the brim with recreational boaters on a long weekend.

Lockman Raymond Laforest conducts a lockage procedure in both official languages. Locking may be simple enough, but filling a lock to accommodate boats of various lengths and widths is an art form that can attract many bystanders for viewing.

Major Phillips transformed the tugs in the floating plant, which consisted of working vessels, into ceremonial Imperial flagships. For his annual inspections in the *Shanly* and *Loretta*, he was accompanied by uniformed staff, including a valet with white gloves, who served the major on the *Loretta* in a specially designed wood-panelled suite. No other employee was permitted to use the airy superintendent's quarters, and most staff slept below decks near the oppressive heat of the boiler.

In the early days of federal control, lockmasters generally came from a family tradition that saw stations handed down from father to son. Between 1867 and 1871, nine lockmaster posts were filled by the son of the previous holder. One of the most common names on the system was Newman. John Newman and his son William ran Nicholson's Locks from 1847 to 1907, while at neighbouring Clowes Locks, Thomas Newman and his son John J. Newman served from 1840 to 1907. When the sons retired they were both rewarded with the Imperial Service Medal, not only for serving for more than thirty-five years, but for continuing in the steps of their fathers, who had helped build the canal as members of the Sappers and Miners.

At Kilmarnock Locks, George Newsome became lockmaster in 1847, and his son William spent a half-century as lockmaster there from 1871 to 1921. For a period of a hundred years, there was always a lockmaster Jones at one of the Smiths Falls stations, probably all of the same family. The last, Arthur S. Jones, put in fifty-eight years of work as a lockman and lockmaster, and was a recipient of the Imperial Service Medal in 1930. Lockmaster Ken Milne of Upper Brewers Locks is a fourth-generation lock worker on the Rideau Canal.

Some of the most dedicated and long-lasting dynasties had to face challenges by members of Parliament seeking patronage plums. In 1896, all lock workers lost their jobs with the change of government, but many were returned to their former positions out of necessity or good sense. In the twentieth century, new rules concerning the civil service, including the affirmative action taken to employ returned veterans after the First World War, affected canal employment. As civil servants, lockmasters were appointed based upon their seniority and skills on the Rideau Canal.

In spite of the advantages of patronage, family ties and military service, a lockmaster normally faced a long ladder from lock labourer to lockman or bridgemaster, and finally to lockmaster. The lockmaster was king of the castle and the notion of being the senior person on a patch of federal land had a dizzying effect on some. One lockmaster at the turn of the century even demanded that an American boat-owner buy a Union Jack at the local general store to replace the offending Stars and Stripes before he would permit lockage. In Perth in 1933, even the lowly bridge-

Single-storey stone defensible lockmaster's houses were built at many stations after the rebellions of 1837–38. Note the musket loopholes in the walls, built to allow those inside to ward off invaders. Lockmaster Peter Sweeney's journal (1839–50) at Jones Falls left an important record that enabled Parks Canada historians and interpreters to restore and recreate the atmosphere of his home as it was in the 1840s.

master could tell the town constable and the strait-laced minister that he had the authority to allow kids to skate at the town basin any time they wanted on a Sabbath day.

Lock stations used to also serve as homes. Licutenant-Colonel John By had originally planned to build blockhouses at every station, to house lock staff and labourers and to be manned by soldiers in time of war. To cut costs, only strategic locks at Kingston Mills, the Narrows, Newboro and Merrickville received blockhouses. The Rebellion of 1837–38 prompted the Ordnance to erect defensible one-storey lockmaster's houses with menacing rifle-slits in the stone walls. Of the few that survive without alterations, the best can be seen at Jones Falls, Old Slys and Davis Lock. Lockmaster's houses were transformed into pastoral dwellings, where families maintained gardens and livestock within a fenced yard. Children received early training on lock chores. Even lockmen lived on site at canal buildings during the navigation season, and carpenter gangs used to take up residence with their own cook when replacing lock gates. Many lock stations were in locations isolated or relatively set apart from villages. Only in Smiths Falls, Merrickville and Ottawa did lockmasters have a sense that they were part of an urban landscape. By the 1960s, because of increased road access and changing lifestyles, many canal staff lived away from their places of work, at least in the off season. When they moved away they took with them some of the welcoming, homey character of the canal.

Then, as now, lockmasters complained about low pay. The most onerous responsibility in the early years was the task of locking boats twenty-four hours a day. When the canal still handled commercial traffic, the locks were never closed except on Sunday. Lockmasters and their staff could be awakened and called to duty at any time of the night. Wives of lockmasters also had their complaints. Clean clothes were pulled in from lines and windows were hastily shut when steamers were passing through, since their noxious fumes and acrid smoke soon enveloped a station. Alice (Thompson) Warren remembered life at Chaffey's Lock in the 1920s and 1930s:

> Although I didn't like the house so dark when we got it painted and papered I got to love the old house, the view was so beautiful looking out over the lake. We were kept very busy, had our cow to milk and we also sold milk and cream and ice to the summer people and we grew all the vegetables we could use. We used coal oil lamps and later got Coleman lamps which was a great help. Then in 1936 they put in Hydro and later we had a bathroom and the electric power allowed us many a luxury as we got an electric washing machine. What a blessing!

Like a lighthouse keeper, a lockmaster had a specific kind of job that existed as a kind of anomaly in general employment. Another important role of a lockmaster on the Rideau Canal was regulating water control. In a slackwater system, dams and water levels have to be maintained to ensure navigable depths upstream and sustain residential and industrial areas downstream. As Superintendent Frederick Wise commented in 1883, because of the complex nature of the Rideau, "more intelligence and judgment [is] required to regulate the water than on the ordinary canals." There is no walking away from this canal It cannot be left a dry channel in the landscape like so many other canals in North America, but must be constantly maintained. The Rideau Canal is part of the watershed and an essential element in the region's biodiversity. The keeper of the gates also has a finger in the dike. Otherwise, the Rideau Canal would have been abandoned long before recreational activity and heritage interests revived its purpose and role.

Sunrise behind Fort Frederick and its Martello tower, the largest of four built in 1846 to defend Kingston's harbour. Point Frederick was once the site of the Royal Dockyard, and the tower now houses the Royal Military College Museum, which celebrates more than a century of military education.

6

KINGSTON: TO PRESERVE AND DEFEND

The Cataraqui River flows sluggishly into the St. Lawrence River and Lake Ontario at Kingston. The LaSalle Causeway and its distinctive bascule bridge mark the canal entrance, although the Kingston Mills locks are located several miles north through broad wetlands that narrow to a gorge. Fort Frontenac, built by the French in 1673 and destroyed by the English in 1758, used to guard the river. To the west of the LaSalle Causeway, Kingston sprawls toward the Bay of Quinte. To the east is Barriefield, overlooking the inner harbour protected by the Royal Military College on Point Frederick and historic Fort Henry.

The British were firmly entrenched when they built fortifications at Fort Cataraqui in 1783, and their numbers increased with the arrival of United Empire Loyalist refugees in 1784. Loyalists under the direction of Sir John Johnson, including Michael Grass, the leader of companies of Associated Loyalists intent on settling at the ruins of the old French fort, and members of the Jessup's Rangers, King's Royal Regiment of New York, King's Rangers, Peter Van Alstine's Associated Loyalists and the Royal Highland Emigrants came to the Cataraqui settlement west of Kingston.

The Rideau Canal did not really create a new focus at Kingston, but fit into an older military establishment originating from the American Revolutionary War and the War of 1812. In the later war the British built a naval dockyard at Point Frederick, reinforced the garrison, and began construction on Fort Henry. Arthur Wesley, Duke of Wellington, advocated a defensive bulwark for Canada that would include forts, garrisons and canals forming a triangle between Montréal, Kingston and a yet-unnamed place, later called Bytown, now Ottawa. In 1825 the Smyth Commission recommended to Wellington that the Rideau Canal be built and fortifications in Kingston be improved. The military essence of the Rideau Canal, particularly at this point where it meets Lake Ontario, survives to this day.

Construction of Fort Henry was finished in 1836, four years after the Rideau Canal was completed. The rebellions of 1837–38 renewed interest in protecting Kingston with a mantle of seaward and landward defences: the four Martello towers were constructed in 1846, and six redoubts were planned but never left the drawing board. The military presence remains even today, at Canadian Forces Base Kingston and at the Royal Military College

The Frontenac County Courthouse, designed by Edward Horsey and built between 1855 and 1858, is just one of many examples of Kingston's architectural heritage.

Loyalist Town, Garrison Town, University Town, or Kings Town–Kingston was also a major centre of trade and commerce in nineteenth-century Ontario. The capital of the Province of Canada from 1841 to 1844, Kingston never lost hope that it would be so honoured in the creation of a new nation. However, at the other end of the Rideau Canal, Slabtown (as Ottawa was then disparagingly known) on the Ottawa River also had capital intentions. The Rideau Canal was only one avenue of economic influence for Kingston. The city looked east down the St. Lawrence to Montreal, west along the lakeshore to Toronto, and south across Lake Ontario to Oswego.

In the early years of the canal, Kingston was a key point in a commercial triangle. Freight and settlers travelled from Montréal up the Ottawa River and through the Rideau Canal to Kingston. At Kingston, goods were transhipped for destinations further west, while freight picked up en route was sent down the St. Lawrence River. This triangle served the Rideau Canal and Kingston well until the improvement of the St. Lawrence canals in the late 1840s lessened the advantages of the Rideau commercial route. Resources were still carried south to Kingston, destined for Oswego, as that trade increased in the 1840s, and Montréal continued to treat the Rideau region as part of its commercial hinterland.

Signs of Kingston's ambitious past survive in several distinctive public buildings, including the county courthouse, city hall and customs house, but the importance and commercial viability of the city had waned even before the remaking of Ontario after Confederation. The centre of the province had been shifting west toward Toronto, and the nature of transhipment changed with transportation systems. What remained was a city ever trying to revive itself in the image it thought it should maintain in the whole province, instead of the limited role it actually played at the eastern end of Lake Ontario.

Barriefield is an important part of the Rideau Canal. Situated across the Cataraqui River from Kingston, the village in Pittsburgh Township was the first area to be designated a Heritage Conservation District by the Ontario Heritage Foundation. Barriefield was a boatbuilders' paradise–a legacy of the naval dockyards at Point Frederick–and several builders there designed recreational boats for cruising the Rideau Canal.

The Loyalist past is reflected in communities north from Kingston Mills. Robert Clark of the Jessup's Rangers helped construct the original Kingston Mills with Robert Brass of the Butler's Rangers in 1783-84. Brass helped rebuild the mills in 1807, and the family name is still associated with Brass Point Bridge at Cranberry Lake. Amos Ansley founded Battersea and the sons of Aaron Brewer developed Brewer's Mills. Their links were with Kingston, but the frontier as it swept northeast from Kingston came under the influence of

"I have taken a cottage or rather, I beg pardon a Villa," wrote John A. Macdonald in 1848, when he rented a house in Kingston, "completely surrounded with trees," with a "fresh breeze ever blowing on it from Lake Ontario." Macdonald, Canada's first prime minister, had from the age of five known several homes in Kingston, but most fondly remembered Bellevue House, at 35 Centre Street, now a National Historic Site maintained by Parks Canada.

The Wolfe Island ferry slides by a waterfront shaped by the towers and domes of Kingston's churches and public buildings.

Fishing lodges and cabins still define a historic fishing tradition on the Rideau. Sunny Acres at Seeley's Bay.

other St. Lawrence settlements. The founders of Seeley's Bay, on an inlet in Cranberry Lake, were Justus and his son John Seeley, early settlers from the Brockville area.

The significant bed of weeds and wetland, known as the greater Cataraqui Marsh, that separates Kingston and Barriefield from the actual entrance locks of the Rideau Canal was a factor in keeping Kingston Mills a distinct, isolated community. Even though it was the site of Eastern Ontario's first mills, a blockhouse, the massive Grand Trunk Railway bridge over the canal entrance, and other important east-west connections, the lock and Kingston Mills never developed as an anchor to the corridor.

The canal served as an avenue to resources, especially before the 1870s when lumbering had largely wiped out local forests. As a transportation corridor, the Rideau Canal did not create the kind of industrial hinterland, at least on the Cataraqui River portion of the canal, that might have attracted more sustained interest from Kingston. The regional railway to the north, the Kingston and Pembroke, followed a path away from the Rideau Canal north to the Ottawa River in the 1880s. The St. Lawrence communities of Gananoque, Brockville, Maitland and Prescott sustained pockets of influence on the Rideau corridor by land that Kingston never did by canal.

The old stones of Kingston and the Rideau's grey stone locks give a sense of a garrison mentality that contrasts with the surrounding pastoral landscapes. The city and canal both had a role in the defence of British North America and both served as gateway to the Great Lakes. But the canal was not a dominant feature of Kingston's broad horizon, and thus affected that city's ongoing life and perspective less than it did in Ottawa.

Seeley's Bay, tucked away in an inlet off Cranberry Lake.

Besides creating a navigable waterway, the Rideau Canal made an intricate pattern of dams and waste weirs, affording opportunities for water-powered industry, including the generation of hydroelectricity. This aerial view shows hydro lines near Jones Falls.

7

THE JONES FALLS DAM

Imagine a wilderness gorge where two hundred men, using little more than their own hands, primitive derricks and straining oxen, excavated and constructed the only arch keywork dam, indeed, a dam twice the size of any in North America and the largest dam in the British Empire at the time. The Brockville *Recorder* in 1830 reported, "The contractor was thrown at once into the heart of the forest, several miles from any settlement, requiring not only great exertion and indefatigable perseverance but a large command of capital to enable him to make a commencement." Much has been written about the engineering skill of Lieutenant-Colonel John By and the Royal Engineers under his command, but most of the canal was actually constructed by contractors such as John Redpath.

At Jones Falls the waters of Sand Lake dropped 60 feet (18.3 m) into Whitefish Lake, through a rugged gorge with steep, rocky banks rising 90 feet (27.5 m) high. Jones Falls would be one of the most daring challenges of the entire system. The arch keywork dam is a marvel of period engineering, stone masonry, construction methods and workmanship. The late historian Robert Legget considered it the masterpiece of Rideau engineering: "In the light of the fact that all the stone was hand cut and hoisted into place by small winches, in the isolation of the Canadian forest, the daring and indeed grandeur of his [Lieutenant-Colonel By's] conception seem all the more remarkable."

Between dam abutments, which were formed by excavating steps into the rocky gorge, the dam stretches 350 feet (107 m) long in a radius of 245 feet (75 m). The stone arch is 62 feet (20 m) high above ground level, and the masonry keywork was sunk 8 feet (2.4 m) into the riverbed to secure a rock foundation. The upstream face of the dam consists of an earth apron extending 127 feet (39 m) out under the water, and a puddle wall containing broken stone grouted with hydraulic cement to make the dam watertight. On the downstream face, blocks of dressed stone 6 feet by 4 feet by 18 inches (1.8 x 1.2 x .5 m) were laid on end in vertical courses that formed a stone arch 27 1/2 feet (8.4 m) thick at the base and 21 1/2 feet (6.5 m) thick at water level. When it was constructed, it shared the distinction with five other high stone arch dams built on the Rideau Canal as the first such dams built in North America, and the Jones Falls dam was just 14 feet (4.3 m) lower than the tallest dam in the world, built in a narrow gorge in Spain.

The high stone arch dam at Jones Falls, the first of its kind and the tallest in North America when built between 1827 and 1832.

Most locks on the Rideau Canal have lifts of from 7 to 10 feet (2 to 3 m), but the set of locks at Jones Falls have lifts of 13 to 15 feet (4 to 4.5 m), the steepest lift of locks on the canal when it opened in 1832. It took four locks at Jones Falls to provide a lift of almost 60 feet (18 m) and eight locks at Ottawa to lift almost 80 feet (24 m).

John Redpath and Thomas McKay were responsible for the contract to build the dam. Scottish immigrants, Redpath and McKay had cut their teeth as contractors on the Lachine Canal in Montréal in the early 1820s. Redpath handled the Jones Falls site. One of McKay's greatest challenges was the Ottawa Locks. While the dam was under construction, they had a work force of two hundred men, including forty stonemasons. McKay went on to found the industrial community of New Edinburgh at Rideau Falls and to construct Rideau Hall, the residence of Canada's governor-general. Redpath returned to Montréal, where he founded Redpath Sugar in 1853.

Next to the Ottawa Locks, Jones Falls is the most-visited lock station on the Rideau Canal, relying on both road and boat traffic. It is home to the famous Hotel Kenney, owned by the same family since 1877. During navigation season, Parks Canada also opens the historic blacksmith shop and the defensible lockmaster's house. Jones Falls is a wonderful place to explore. Trails wind their way around the dam, turning basin, bridge, four locks and historic buildings. Here one has a real sense of the grandeur and magnificence of the Rideau Canal.

A proud little stone grist-mill, now a residence, is almost all that remains of the industrial ghost town of Bedford Mills, snuggled below Buttermilk Falls between Devil Lake and Loon Lake.

8

BEDFORD MILLS

On County Road 10, better known as the Perth Road, close to the eastern boundary of Frontenac County in Bedford Township, is a little ghost town almost completely hidden from view. Driving south alongside the marshes of Loon Lake and looking west, one catches a brief glimpse of the beautiful stone Bedford Mill. This restored mill, now a residence, anchors the remains of a once-thriving mill village at the base of Buttermilk Falls. The site also makes a picturesque setting for the quaint St. Stephen's Anglican Church, which was built in 1905.

Bedford Mills is no longer considered accessible from the channel of the Rideau Canal, except by canoe, but it is very much part of the Rideau Waterway. When the lock station at Chaffey's was completed in 1832, it created reservoirs in Clear, Indian, Newboro, Mosquito (later Opinicon) and Loon Lakes that gave a shallow and weedy access to the base of Buttermilk Falls, an ancient outlet for a series of lakes from the west (some within the boundary of Frontenac Provincial Park). Nearby rivers and streams once flowed in the spring with timber cut from the surrounding forests. Dams were also maintained here to control the water feeding the Rideau Canal, and later, to serve hydroelectric development.

Benjamin Tett, who emigrated from Somerset, England, in 1820, residing first in Perth and later in Newboro, was the individual most responsible for the development of Bedford Mills. Excited by canal construction and the market and access it created, Tett was sawing lumber by 1829, and sending squared timber to Québec markets. Tett also worked as a general merchant in Newboro and helped supply wheat to canal contractor Thomas McKay's mill complex at the outlet of the Rideau River at New Edinburgh.

Benjamin Tett was nearly driven into bankruptcy in 1846 when he couldn't sell squared timber that had been rafted to Québec. A severe recession and the loss of preferential duties for Canadian timber in Great Britain were straining the overseas market. Tett formed a partnership with the Chaffey family, who expanded the original sawmill in 1847 and built the surviving grist mill by 1850. The Chaffeys capitalized on the growing American lumber market via the Rideau Canal, Kingston, Oswego and the Erie Canal. The rough-and-tumble community boasted wharves, lumber yards, a blacksmith shop, boarding house and sleeping annex.

Samuel and Benjamin Chaffey, sons of an English woollens manufacturer, arrived in Upper Canada in 1816 and established themselves in the mercantile trade on the St. Lawrence River. They were attracted in 1820 to the Cataraqui River corridor, where they established a milling complex, including a sawmill and grist mill, a brewery, and a carding and fulling mill. Samuel Chaffey died in 1827, and when the lock station was later constructed on the mill site, it was named after him. Benjamin Chaffey's sons, William, John (who married Tett's daughter), and George, maintained their interest in milling, lumbering, forwarding and boatbuilding and found their partnership with Benjamin Tett a convenient arrangement.

Lumbering before Confederation was a way of life to the people of the Rideau. Shantymen headed into the bush in late fall to construct their camboose shanties, which were large temporary bunkhouses distinguished by a central open-hearth fire pit approximately 10 feet (3 m) square, set below a large log chimney that provided light and ventilation and carried away most of the smells of smoke, soiled clothes and unwashed men. The rough-hewn, rectangular building of horizontal pine logs often had a floor sunk below grade, thus exposing less wall to winter storms, and the buildings were almost buried by snowdrifts, providing extra protection from drafts that seeped through the moss chinking in the wall. Roofing material was constructed of hollowed-out half-logs, the first layer forming scoops or troughs with the hollow side up and a second set placed on top with the hollow side down. The fire was always blazing, providing light, warmth and heat for cooking. Out of the cool, dimly lit lumber shanties came a distinctive tradition of song and lyrics about hauling down the pine.

Lumbermen bearing axes were sent out in gangs to cut trees into sawlogs or squared timber. Teams using oxen or horses sledded the timber over rude snow-roads to shoreline dumps. At spring runoff, logs and timber were pushed into swollen streams and guided by nimble rivermen to places such as Buttermilk Falls. On the Rideau Canal, square timber was formed into drams, or lock "bands," to be towed through the locks, while sawlogs were barged or driven through waste weirs around dams. Lumber sawn at the mill was loaded onto barges to be towed by Tett tugs. Irish and Scottish immigrants, French Canadians, and during the winter, local farmers, made up the work force in the forest, while the mills employed men as long as there was water to drive the machinery. Bedford Mills was but a small part of the lumbering empire that devoured the legendary forests of the Ottawa River and Great Lakes watersheds of the nineteenth century. In 1850 the sawmill at Bedford Mills, with twenty "gang saws," cut and exported to New York markets almost two million board-feet of

Benjamin Tett's house, post office and general store, built at Newboro in the 1830s.

Deep in the bowels of the Canadian Shield, at Murphy's Point Provincial Park in North Burgess Township, visitors may enter the historic Silver Queen mica mine, which operated between 1903 and 1920.

white pine. In all, more than eight million board-feet of lumber were exported in 1850 from Bedford Mills, the Angus Cameron sawmill built at Kingston Mills in 1847, and Robert Anglin's sawmill at Brewers Mills. These mills more than doubled their output later in the decade, but by the 1870s, good merchantable timber was growing scarce.

Benjamin Tett had always held public office from his days in Perth, and in Newboro he rose to the position of reeve in North Crosby Township. He was a member of the pre-Confederation provincial legislature in 1857 and the first legislature of Ontario in 1867. The partnership with the Chaffey family was severed in 1871, and Tett's sons John Poole and Benjamin Jr. assumed responsibility for Bedford Mills in 1872.

The Tetts continued forwarding goods on the canal with their own vessels, and expanded their business, so that by 1880 there were eighty people living at Bedford Mills and the community had its own post office. They found markets for railway ties and cordwood, encouraged dairying and established a cheese factory, and in 1899 fitted the grist mill with new roller machinery to create a finer brand of flour. Local deposits of phosphate and mica sustained considerable interest in mining in the area from 1870 to 1914, but deposits tended to be shallow and operations small. One such operation was the Silver Queen Mine, which is open for visitors at Murphy's Point Provincial Park.

Dwindling forest reserves, a changing wheat economy, and isolation from urban areas eroded the function of many small resource centres such as Bedford Mills even before the twentieth century. Forwarding on the canal declined as other areas felt the effects of similar economic changes, including rural depopulation and the centralization of manufacturing into larger urban areas. By the 1920s the mills were closed, and when Edmund Tett built a small hydroelectric generating plant at the falls, the old sawmill was demolished.

The stillness of Bedford Mills is now broken only in the spring when the former mill and hydro-plant sluices are filled to overflowing. The torrent gives some idea of the power and beauty of the original Buttermilk Falls. Modern Bedford Mills only hints at its once-frenetic pace as a mill site, but it is a reminder of the resources that helped sustain the commercial viability of the region, and the web of interconnection created by a canal and its watershed.

At Cranberry Lake the Rideau Canal rises into the Frontenac Axis of the Canadian Shield, where ancient bedrock and mixed forest define a rugged landscape of lakes and islands.

9

THE DROWNED LANDS

The Rideau is not an ordinary fishing ground. Unlike many of the lakes and rivers of cottage country's near north, the Rideau Waterway is an almost completely altered habitat. The building of the canal created drowned lands and marshes, tamed rapids and waterfalls, and turned rivers into a chain of lakes and reaches separated by locks and dams. The construction of the Rideau Canal upset the ancient ecological balance; we can only imagine the changes by observing rivers that have been more recently altered.

The Cataraqui River likely experienced the most radical change. The lands once surrounding the string of lakes known as Sand, Opinicon, Indian, Clear and Newboro, when flooded, became a series of bass pools that would later be renowned in North American fishing lore. In 1911 Justice Kelly Evans wrote in his *Report of the Ontario Game and Fisheries Commission*, "Perhaps the best fishing grounds...in the Province occur in the drowned lands to be found along the Rideau Lake system, and it would be hard, indeed, to discover waters more admirably adapted to the requirements alike of the fish and the bait-caster." Where the waters of the dammed Cataraqui River rose, a forest of dead trees stood submerged in sections of the new lakes. Over the next half-century, the trunks rotted and the wind scattered the skeletons into the shallow waters, creating an ideal habitat for the largemouth bass, a prized fish species. By the 1870s the tangled underwater forests evolved into remarkably rich and fertile bass fishing grounds.

American fishermen seeking ever more alluring backwaters were attracted by the growing reputation of the area. The St. Lawrence River was becoming one of the favourite recreational areas on the continent by the 1860s and 1870s, and the construction of the Brockville, Westport and Pacific Railway (it never got beyond Westport) from 1884 to 1888 gave the Rideau immediate accessibility from the south.

Clint Fleming, author of *When the Fish Are Rising: Tales of the Rideau Lakes* (1947), commented on fishing on the Rideau in the late nineteenth century: "I have a picture, taken about that time, of four men standing in back of a catch of one hundred and fifty-four bass, not one of which was under three pounds, and all taken by that grinning foursome in a single day's fishing."

The mill at Chaffey's Lock in late fall. Built by John Chaffey in 1870, it has been altered several times and, along with the lock and fishing lodges, is a continuing landmark in the village.

The mill at Chaffey's Lock in spring freshet.

Lodges and small hotels, many no more than private homes, started catering to fishermen in the 1860s. The Hotel Kenney at Jones Falls, dating from 1877 (and still in the family), was moved closer to the river in the 1890s where it could improve on its character as a tourist resort. Simmons Lodge was begun at Chaffey's Lock with a single guest in 1886. Newboro had several hotels, but the Rideau Hotel, now Stirling Lodge, was from the early 1890s a distinctive fishing resort. The former home of W.H. Fredenburgh, merchant, miller and forwarder of Westport, was transformed in 1929 into the Lexina Hotel, later the Tweedsmuir, and now part of the Cove Country Inn. From 1899, the Opinicon Hotel (originally Idlywilde) at Chaffey's Lock went through several stages of expansion on both sides of John Chaffey's house to become the largest fishing resort in the area. Described in the *Pittsburgh Press* in 1944 as "a resort purely for fishermen and their ladies," the Opinicon welcomed more than half of its guests between 1907 and 1955 from the United States, especially New York and Ohio. Some vistors found accomodation at large resorts at places such as Portland and Rideau Ferry and many others stayed at smaller establishments with fishing cabins.

Since the drowned lands were a nightmare for early boaters, guides were hired by the hotels, or by individual fishermen, to take them to their favourite locations. Local boatbuilders refined the double-ended rowing skiff, which developed on the St. Lawrence River, for the more placid waters of the Rideau. Fishermen were taken to their grounds in their skiffs as part of a tow involving several boats and a lead steam yacht, or later, a motor launch. They could all be locked through at the same time, and would unhitch themselves from the train as they approached their areas, to be picked up again for the return to lodge or hotel.

Clint Fleming remembered the early morning atmosphere: "With a score of lakes that can be fished from Chaffey's Locks, it is customary to see upward of fifty boats setting out each morning. It is the liveliest time of the day. There are always new faces; the guides are busy stowing away lunchbaskets and arranging skiffs for towing. Hopes are high, no matter what the previous day's luck has been, and there is a feeling of excitement and goodfellowship in the air."

The guides in the region were drawn from throughout the area, especially Chaffey's Lock, Elgin, Jones Falls, Morton, Newboro, and Westport. They were expert fishermen, great cooks, and often, accomplished boatbuilders. In most cases the guide provided a skiff, live bait and a lunch (fried fish, Canadian bacon, French toast, boiled potatoes, dessert and piping-hot coffee), and would row one or two fishermen around what was hoped would be a prime fishing area.

Guiding fishermen to the best haunts of the bass involved much more than fish talk.

The Opinicon verandah evokes comfort and relaxation, a tradition of fishing holidays on the Rideau Waterway. Opened as Idlewilde in 1899, the Opinicon still maintains a rich atmosphere of backwoods adventure.

Drowned lands at the Narrows Lock

As Clint Fleming recalled, "Long ago, I was foolish enough to think that an expert knowledge of fishing was all I needed to be a successful guide. But I soon found that was less than half of it; when a man engages you to take him fishing, he takes it for granted that you can and will get him fish. In addition, you've got to be a good cook, a philosopher, and a patient, sympathetic listener when the customers begin to unburden themselves to you. And most of them do. The troubles I have listened to in twenty years! And the advice I've given!"

The many talents and skills of these guides sustained a sport fishery and recreational style that brought fishermen back to the region for years, indeed, for generations. Guiding was not limited to the Jones Falls–Newboro corridor, but it found its greatest expression and character in that region.

There are still signs of that early era on this section of the canal. The Stirling Lodge, Hotel Kenney and Opinicon Hotel give a sense of backwoods adventure with a dash of elegance and Rideau simplicity. Their rooms seem to echo with the tall tales and banter of an earlier era. The guides are mostly gone, as are most of the sleek wooden skiffs, and the railway to Westport and Chaffey's Lock (which arrived at the latter in 1913). The popularity and convenience of the motorboat eventually removed much of the mystery and adventure of fishing and boating. Everyone is now his or her own guide, and the secrets of bass fishing are more widely shared.

The deep waters of Big Rideau Lake enticed lake trout fishermen from far and wide (a commercial whitefish and trout fishery survived there until the 1970s), and the muskie on the Long Reach of the Rideau River are still viable but threatened. Nearly every lockmaster can tell stories of great catches, right off the locks, of pike, bass or pickerel. In open seasons, dams and lock reaches are often crowded with ardent fishermen, especially at Kilmarnock Lock.

Numerous fishing contests, pro-bass tournaments, and fishing lodges are superficial signs of the viability of Rideau fishing. However, the presence of the loon, the great blue heron and the osprey are also evidence that fish are abundant. Lieutenant-Colonel By's plans helped form a perfect habitat for certain species of fish, but continuing management is essential to sustain the Rideau system as a living environment for fish and the organisms they thrive on. There may be enough limestone to counter some of the effects of acid rain, but there must be more determined effort to protect our wetlands and counteract the effects of human waste, shoreline erosion and pollutants on our waterways.

Don Warren rowing his Wykes skiff through the drowned lands of Lake Opinicon, in front of his home. The Warren family were on the Cataraqui River before the canal, and their dedication to the natural and cultural heritage of the Rideau Canal has increased awareness of its special role in Eastern Ontario.

10

DON WARREN
DEFENDER OF THE RIDEAU

Don Warren is one of the reasons the Rideau Canal is a Heritage Canal. Just before the celebration of Canada's Centennial in 1967, the Department of Transport, then operating the Rideau Canal, embarked on a scheme to modify several lock stations for electrical operation. Warren was the leader of a public interest group, the Rideau Action Association, formed to save Rideau lock stations from modernization. The Black Rapids and Newboro lock stations were electrified in 1966 and 1968 respectively, and the Smiths Falls Combined Locks were rebuilt as a single electrified lock by 1972. Warren and his associates drew the line at Chaffey's Lock. "We raised hell all over," Don Warren says, "They were going to celebrate one hundred years of Confederation by wrecking the canal."

Don Warren had good reason to be upset at the planned automation and electrification of the Rideau Canal. Born and raised on the locks, he knew that the historical character of the Rideau was one of the reasons it was such an important landmark. The Warren family arrived in the Chaffey's Lock area at least fifteen years before 1832, the year the Rideau Canal was completed. Don's father, Herman Warren of Clear Lake, was injured in 1918 at the Battle of Cambrai in northern France during the First World War while fighting with the Princess Patricia's Canadian Light Infantry. As a returned veteran he was accepted for employment on the Rideau Canal at Newboro Lock where he became lockman, and he married Alice Thompson in 1919. Don Warren was born at the lock station in 1921; his father was promoted to lockmaster at Chaffey's Lock in 1929.

Don Warren got to know the Rideau channel and its shores, and at age fourteen he was accepted into the unofficial fraternity of local fishing guides, taking up a post at the Opinicon. The Second World War interrupted, and Warren was trained as a line and wireless operator, serving overseas. Upon his return, he attended Queen's University and the Ontario College of Education. He took a second job as a high-school teacher and was still guiding when head of the English Department at Kingston Collegiate and Vocational Institute. Warren was so attached to the Chaffey's Lock area that he drew a circle of 100-mile radius on a map with the lock at its centre and said he would not teach beyond that circle. It must have surprised many an American fisherman

A dam at Smiths Falls. The Rideau Canal is a water-control system where seasonal adjustments are made at waste weirs and overflow dams to help control flooding in spring, maintain water levels during the navigation season, and regulate water flow for urban, industrial, and hydroelectric generating purposes.

who thought he had hired an upcountry Canuck guide to receive a lecture about the proper use of the King's English.

The Warren family purchased the Regan farm on Opinicon Lake in 1968, just in time to take on the Department of Transport and its modernization plans. The efforts of Don Warren and his neighbours helped spur the transfer of control of the Rideau Canal to more sensitive and caring hands at Parks Canada. The change took place at a time when lockmaster's houses were no longer being used for year-round residence, and Warren formed the Chaffey's Lock Improvement Committee to save his boyhood home from alterations that would have changed its character. The result was the creation of the lockmaster's house museum operated by the Chaffey's Lock and Area Heritage Society.

The Warren residence is a good place to learn about stewardship, the responsibility for keeping the shoreline a living, thriving environment. Aside from maintaining a young forest under an agreement with the provincial

Rack and pinion gears, etched into the horizon, were installed to operate sluices located within the lower lock-gates at lock stations.

government, and preserving areas of wetland deep in one of Opinicon Lake's most remote drowned lands, Don Warren leaves a shoreline rich in natural profusion. The Warrens receive accolades from experts and students sent to their property to observe wildlife from neighbouring Queen's University Biological Station.

Residents on the Rideau corridor have long been wary of changes and upgrades that threatened the integrity of the canal and its environment. Even in the 1930s, Don Warren's mother, Alice, remembered the historic swing-bridge across the locks. "How I hated to see the old wooden one go, it seemed to fit in with the beauty of the lock." The Warrens have always acknowledged the need to renew lock and canal structures, but they championed the preservation of operating methods and the distinctive character of the Rideau Canal experience. Don Warren played a significant role in the 150th celebrations of the Rideau Canal in 1982 and is an honourary member of the Rideau Waterway Co-ordinating Association, known as the Friends of the Rideau.

The Best family arrived in 1820 to farm on Big Rideau Lake, upstream from Rideau Ferry near McVeety's Bay, and this simple stone vernacular building is still in family hands as a cottage. The family believes the house may date from the 1850s, but it would have had to have escaped a vast fire that spread along the north shore of the Rideau Lakes in 1870.

11

RIDEAU LAKES COTTAGES

The Rideau Lakes cottage community stretches 45 miles (72 km) from Cranberry Lake in the south to Lower Rideau Lake in the north. Some of the largest cottage clusters on the Rideau Canal are found here, and some communities, such as Chaffey's Lock, Newboro, Portland-on-the Rideau, Seeley's Bay, Rideau Ferry and Westport, are now largely defined by their recreational role even though based on earlier village foundations.

Many other Ontario cottage communities in regional lakelands are confined and defined by a single lake or group of lakes, but the pattern of land use and recreational development on the Rideau Lakes, as in the Kawarthas, has been shaped by a canal. The Rideau waters were affected by other rivers, lakes and navigation systems, especially the St. Lawrence River.

Except for Lower Rideau Lake, between Rideau Ferry and Poonamalie, which is characterized by the Smiths Falls limestone plain, the Rideau Lakes lie within the Frontenac Axis of the Canadian Shield. The Rideau Lakes recreational area can easily be divided into two parts at the headwaters of the two river systems that make up the Rideau Waterway. The Cataraqui River section, below Newboro, was influenced by American sports fishermen from the 1860s and 1870s, and also by the access created by the Brockville, Westport and Pacific Railway opened in 1888.

On the Rideau River system, Lower Rideau, Big Rideau and Upper Rideau Lakes were influenced by their proximity to the developing towns of Perth, Smiths Falls and Ottawa. The earliest cottagers on these lakes were townspeople who found easy access by way of canal to the lakeshore and numerous islands. In 1889 the Ontario Crown Lands Department surveyed the islands of Big Rideau Lake, and numbered and made them available for sale or lease. The early 1880s were boom years in Rideau Valley towns such as Perth and Smiths Falls. The Southern Ontario main line of the Canadian Pacific Railway was being built through the towns between Montréal and Toronto, and mills and manufacturing firms were being opened or expanded with a new-found confidence associated with Prime Minister John A. Macdonald's National Policy. The Tay Canal was revived in three stages between 1882 and 1891. Increased prosperity and time away from work for the emerging middle class, and a sense of enervating revival associated with lakes and forests, led many to the Rideau Canal. They came by way of

In the Evans family since 1916, the Pines, on Big Rideau Lake opposite Fancy Free Island, boasts a boathouse over fifty years old that has survived to high-water levels, ice and the elements. Clusters of boathouses near towns and villages were eradicated by canal and local authorities after the 1930s because of fire hazards and poor maintenance, eventually giving rise to the marina tradition on the Rideau.

steamer excursions and private boats, planned picnics, set up camps, visited resorts and built cottages.

Thomas Hicks Sr. was a Perth carriage-maker with a growing family when he decided to build a small cottage near the newly built Beveridges Locks in the 1880s. It was a small place for the family to get away from town, just a short distance down the Tay River. For almost forty years the Hicks family enjoyed their holidays on the Rideau. In 1918, the eldest son, Thomas Jr., decided to buy property, which they would call Pethern Point, farther up the lake beyond Rideau Ferry. Thomas Hicks Jr. had worked in New York and there admired the Adirondacks, and he had also worked in British Columbia, where he discovered the beauty of red cedar. His new two-storey log chateau was a masterpiece, built by Milford Rabb and Wesley James from B.C. cedar in the style of an Adirondack cottage with Finnish influences. Built on a peninsula under canopies of pine, beech, basswood and maple, and facing soft southwesterly breezes, the cottage offered the sense of isolation the family sought, yet was accessible to Perth by way of rural roads in summer and ice roads in winter.

The Hicks were so pleased with their lakeland retreat that they took early retirement, altered the building for winterization in 1923, and moved in to live there year-round for the next twenty-five years. They became self-sufficient for many of their supplies, and after

Western red cedar and Finnish design techniques were used in the construction of Pethern Point Cottage in 1919, built to resemble hunting and fishing lodges seen in the Adirondack forest by Perth-born Thomas Norman Hicks.

Probably the oldest still-standing cottage on Big Rideau Lake, dating from the 1870s, Fancy Free once hosted Sunday religious services for lake campers and is now owned by the Gould and Burger families.

closing down the carriage shop, moved portions of the building, machinery and hardware to the lake, where Thomas and his brother William set up shop building skiffs, furniture, distinctive lamps and shades, and even manufacturing their own patented battery-powered flashlights. Designed as a cottage and evolved into a home, the building has since reverted to cottage under the ownership of direct descendants, including the Dickinson, Turner, Roelofson, Hathaway and Canning families.

Between the 1890s and 1920s, town boats in Perth and Smiths Falls served the recreational market, transporting passengers and package freight as well as providing excursions for those who could not afford a powerboat or found it too hard to paddle or row out to the lakes. Families with cottages or at camps could predict the arrival of working fathers on Friday evening by watching the lanterns signalling the approach of the late boat glide along distant docks as men disembarked.

The first gasoline-powered motorboats arrived on the Rideau in 1901 and soon transformed the nature of recreational activity on the lakes. Although steamship companies had connections with railways at Ottawa, Kingston, Smiths Falls, Perth, Newboro and Westport from the 1880s, they never formed the kinds of transportation alliances that existed in other lake communities. The one exception was that formed between the New York Central Railway and the Rideau Lakes Navigation Company in 1899. The Northern Railway, with stations in Chaffey's Lock, Portland and Smiths Falls en route from Toronto to Ottawa in 1913, contributed to the demise of lake steamers. By the 1920s, improved road access and the growing popularity of the motorboat made passenger steamers a rare sight on the waterway.

Present-day cottage communities are much more diverse than were the original clusters. Although renovations have changed the character of earlier cottages, the pagoda style of building is common. These cottages developed over time, beginning with a short, squat, rectangular or square clapboard building, then acquiring a surrounding verandah, which would eventually be filled in, and then enlarged by adding on another open verandah. Along the roofline the original structure is visible, expanded by ever-extending verandahs that were never part of the original design.

The Rideau Lakes have rugged shorelines and are pocketed with deep bays; they contain a myriad of islands and several significant wetlands. Except for a few small locations, shoreline development is dispersed and has little effect on the character of the surrounding forest. The Rideau has thus far avoided extensive development pressures, but it will be a challenge to retain the character of the lakes and still allow the kinds of changes that have been occuring since the canal opened in 1832.

The Ottawa International Antique and Classic Boat Show, held each year in August, is hosted by the Manotick Classic Boat Club at several locations, including Westport on Upper Rideau Lake.

12

POLISHED MAHOGANY AND GLEAMING BRASS

Some people, thinking of their earliest memories, recall a favourite stuffed toy. Jimmy Potter remembers the feel of mahogany and the splash of the Rideau wake. In 1938, the same year his parents were married, they commissioned a new boat to be built by the Gilbert Boat Company of Brockville. Soon after they got the boat, Jimmy came along. Jimmy was followed by a new baby, *Riot*, a 20-foot twin-cockpit Peterborough purchased in 1940, and then by *Riot II*, an exceptionally fast 18-foot twin-cockpit runabout with a V-bottom, powered by a St. Lawrence Marine V-8 Ford conversion engine.

The Potters farmed near Manotick where their ancestors had settled in 1842. They started a milk supply business, and built a cottage on Big Rideau Lake. Jimmy Potter went into the business of restoring boats as an adjunct to the milk transportation operation he inherited from his father. In 1965, he joined with John Millar and formed Millar-Potter Restorations Ltd. It was only natural that Potter would become a founding member and first president of the Manotick Classic Boat Club in 1976. The club was formed as a social group for people who had an interest in the early wooden boat tradition and became a society devoted to the restoration and preservation of classic and antique boats.

Potter can remember the thrill of the Rideau Ferry and Portland regattas. Although the Rideau Ferry regatta can be traced to 1897, before the advent of the gasoline-powered motorboat on the Rideau in 1901, it was the motorboat races and challenges that most thrilled the crowds. The regattas suffered from the introduction of mass-market fibreglass and aluminum boats; wooden boats built by Myles Jeffrey used to compete in their own event, but there was no sense of competition among brand-name boat owners. Expediency ruled a burgeoning market where craftsmanship and style were displaced by economies of construction and mass production.

However, if cared for, wooden boats last forever. The craft of wooden boatbuilding has not been lost; it survived as an art form, preserved by enthusiasts such as Jimmy Potter and John Millar. They devised a conservation strategy to rescue neglected wooden boats from ignominious fates. Out of the boathouses and storage sheds of Rideau cottages came the originals, restored to their former glory.

Cruising the Rideau Canal are boats from interconnecting inland waterways from all over eastern North America.

Just as the Adirondacks, the Muskoka Lakes and the St. Lawrence River had their own boatbuilding traditions, so too did the Rideau. As part of a waterway that linked different traditions and served many functions, the Rideau Canal was home to an eclectic variety of wooden vessels. Rideau boatbuilders devised plans of their own and borrowed from other traditions to create their own styles. Dowsett of Portland, Nichol of Smiths Falls, Dey of Ottawa, Knapp of Barriefield, Harold of Rideau Ferry, Conley of Westport, Mason of Smiths Falls, Patterson of Elgin, Alford of Chaffey's Locks, Lindsay of Kars, and many others crafted boats for the Rideau, often just a handful in a year. Also associated with the Rideau were builders on the Ottawa and St. Lawrence Rivers and regional builders such as Myles Jeffrey of Athens.

Recreational boats were introduced on the Rideau by members of the Royal Engineers who ventured out into the marshes in search of wildfowl and fish. Steam yachts made their appearance in the 1870s at about the same time as the early models of the St. Lawrence skiff. Canoes had always been used and sailing boats were adaptable to the inner lakes. In 1901 the first boat powered by the internal combustion engine was launched in the Tay Basin at Perth. Recreational boating breathed new life into the Rideau Canal.

Leisure boating in the late nineteenth century was largely associated with the public adventure of the excursion vessel, but the motorboat satisfied the desire of many for a more private recreational experience. As motorboats made private properties accessible and convenient, many large hotels soon gave way to private camps and cottages. The Rideau Waterway increased in importance as a recreational facility as hotels and fishing camps were joined by, and outnumbered by, private cottages, boathouses and marinas.

The Rideau Canal was perfectly suited for public and private recreational boating. In Ottawa, the canal served not only to provide access to the city, but also as a site for such places as the Rideau Canoe Club. Rowing, canoeing, sailing and other boating excursions were popular pastimes. Before the automobile improved access to the interior lakes, the Ottawa section of the Rideau Canal was dominated by hundreds of boathouses and several large marinas where Ottawa's middle class stored their personal visas to the waterway. As more cottages took root, more vessels were stored on-site.

The Manotick Classic Boat Club operates the annual Ottawa International Classic and Antique Boat Show every August. The event attracts thousands to such Rideau locations as Ottawa, Merrickville, Westport, Portland, Rideau Ferry and Perth. There you will see an outstanding selection of wooden recreational boats, including many that were built on the Rideau Waterway.

The town-hall clock on Perth's Gore Street symbolizes the pursuit of trade, tourism and administration in the bustling downtown, but artist Sandy McNulty's cow in the window of the local butcher shop is a reminder of Perth's continuing role as a farmers' market.

13

PERTH ON THE TAY

The town of Perth has a history that parallels that of the Rideau Canal. Perth came to be because of the expectation that a canal would be built. At some time in their histories, both were considered off the beaten track, but had powerful influences beyond their immediate territory; both were cloaked in a garrison-like military respectability, and yet survived threatened redundancy to thrive again in the light of heritage awareness. The town of Perth and the Rideau Canal each retain some original structures and operating mechanisms (Perth's motto is Make Haste Slowly), and each has passed through several evolutionary stages with many physical and cultural influences intact.

Like the canal, Perth was the invention of government. Created as the first depot of the Rideau military settlement in 1816, it had by 1823 become the administrative centre for the large Bathurst District, which contained such satellites as Ottawa and Renfrew. Once the preserve of military officers on half-pay pensions, Perth became a magnet for a mercantile, legal and judicial elite who constructed grand edifices considered appropriate to their standing in the worlds of trade, commerce and administration. Many of these buildings and storefronts continue to grace the town and provide a character and style that has won national recognition.

Because much of the land along the Rideau corridor had been gobbled up by absentee landlords, mostly United Empire Loyalists awarded huge grants after 1784, Perth was located at a portage site on the Tay River about 9 miles (15 km) upstream from the projected path of the canal through the Rideau Lakes. When the Rideau Canal was under construction, local half-pay officer, magistrate, merchant and assemblyman William Morris campaigned to construct a private canal on the Tay River. He used funds raised through the joint-stock Tay Navigation Company, through the sale of lots on Cockburn Island in the middle of Perth, and through grants from business and government. The result by 1834 was a little canal twisting through marsh and five shallow locks from Perth to present-day Port Elmsley. As a private venture, the company hoped that tolls would not only sustain maintenance costs but raise the capital needed to build a better system in the future. The canal did not meet such rosy expectations and was largely treated as a timber slide by the 1840s when lumbering was in its heyday.

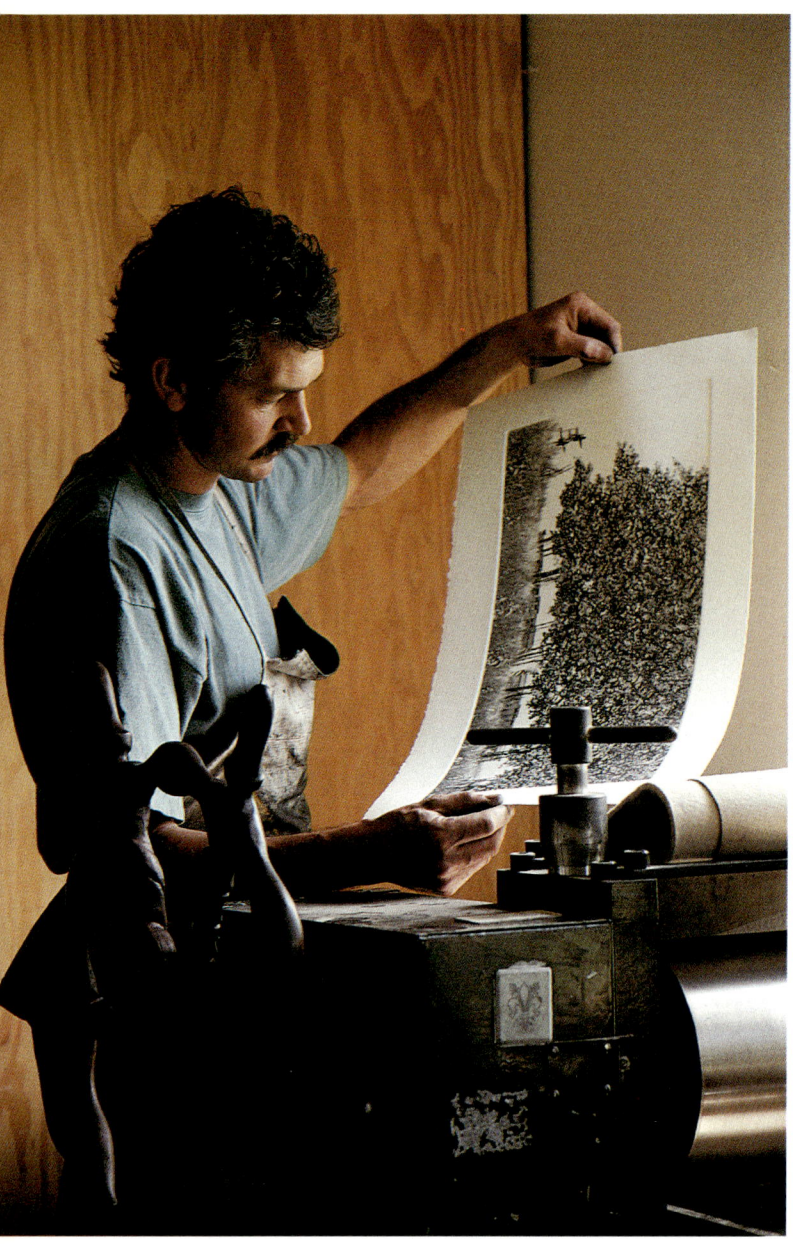

The Rideau corridor is a magnet for artisans and artists. Frank Van Oort, near Perth, is one of many who have found their niche in the region. Annual craft fairs, art shows and workshop tours are conducted throughout the area, especially at Merrickville, Perth and Westport.

The Tay Canal under construction near Perth was the site of Canada's last fatal duel, on 13 June, 1833, when students-at-law John Wilson and Robert Lyon tried to shoot each other over Lyon's alleged slight to the character of Elizabeth Hughes, who was later to be Wilson's wife. Lyon died and Wilson, who was aquitted for having adopted "the only alternative which men of honour thought open," went on to serve many years as a judge in Ontario Courts of Common Pleas. Duelling had become a nasty honour-bound tradition in Perth society, especially among Perth's first three lawyers, Family Compact Tory James Boulton, Reformer Thomas M. Radenhurst and Loyalist Daniel McMartin. Several times they or their families challenged each other in duels; Wilson and Lyon were students of Boulton and Radenhurst respectively. Most interestingly, the houses of the duelling families still stand south of the Tay. Boulton's Summit House shared the highest point in town, of course, with the courthouse; McMartin's ostentatious, cupola-adorned Federal-style pile at Gore and Harvey Streets announced his presence quite effectively; and Radenhurst's Inge-Va is a Rideau classic displayed in a parklike setting, also on Harvey Street. The buildings shared a Georgian classicism, each with different architectural details, reflecting attitudes prevalent in Upper Canada social hierarchy, but revealing none of the tensions that once drove men to fight duels of honour.

Cora Lavender Wellman sits by her faithful kitchen stove in a house her father built on the site of the old Tay Navigation Company office in Port Elmsley. Her Irish forebears helped construct Poonamalie Lock on the Rideau Canal.

Perth's early character was influenced by Scots who arrived as part of an assisted emigration scheme at the same time as the military settlers. However, as early as 1842, the Irish were the dominant ethnic group in town. The strong agricultural community, based on the Perth clay plain, helped sustain the local economy as the lumber frontier moved farther up the Ottawa Valley. Perth's circle of influence grew smaller with boundary changes, but it continued its role as county town for Lanark. It had neither the sustained water-power nor the railway connections critical to expansion that sped the growth of other Lanark County towns such as Almonte, Carleton Place and Smiths Falls. However, in the early 1880s Perth received a significant boost with the construction of the Canadian Pacific Railway between Montréal and Toronto and the revival of the Tay Canal.

John Graham Haggart, who served forty-one years as the Conservative member for South Lanark in Parliament, was an expert at delivering political plums. Just before the federal elections of 1882, 1887 and 1891, Haggart arranged timely announcements about new stages in the construction of the second Tay Canal. The new canal was ostensibly required to improve water control on the Rideau Canal and to transport bulk freight from anticipated

Horses have been at the centre of Perth Fair activities for 150 years, and never more so than now, with equestrian Ian Millar as a local resident. In this photograph a woman competes in one of many events held over the Labour Day weekend.

mining and smelting ventures. The canal created a new channel by-passing Port Elmsley to Beveridges Bay on Lower Rideau Lake, where two Rideau Canal standard locks were constructed by 1887. The canal was pushed to the old Tay Basin, which was also widened by 1890, but the bubble burst in 1891 when Opposition members noted in Parliament that John Haggart was promoting an extension of Haggart's Ditch (as the canal was then known) to Haggart's Island so that the steamer *John Haggart* could travel to Haggart's flour mill. Haggart was rewarded with the portfolio of Minister of Railways and Canals the same year.

The publicly financed second Tay Canal was no better a commercial success than the privately financed first Tay Canal. However, the new canal was opened just as the Rideau Canal was reviving as a place for recreational boating, camping, fishing and cottaging. The Tay Canal offered recreational access to the heart of Perth and the Rideau Lakes, giving the region a new lease on life. Town boats, usually dual-purpose steam yachts or stubby little steamers, provisioned the Rideau Lakes recreational market and conducted excursions from Perth and Smiths Falls from the 1890s to the 1920s. Several larger Rideau steamers, including the *Rideau King* and *Rideau Queen*, vintage examples of Edwardian opulence containing staterooms, saloons and dining rooms, also operated between Kingston and Ottawa during the same period.

At the beginning of the twentieth century, Perth attracted several branch plants at the edge of town, offering a diverse range of products. Perth's two famous distilleries, John A. McLaren's, and Spalding and Stewart's, were closed as a result of temperance legislation in 1916, and the site of McLaren's was developed after 1925 as Stewart Park, a delightful public place in the heart of town. Perth's relatively slow growth in mid-century saved the core of the town from extensive alterations, and its heritage and main-street character has inspired present-day conservation and preservation. Perth was at the centre of attention as a Heritage Canada pilot project for main-street renewal in 1980 and is presently in the initial stages of the Perth Theatre Project to revive the Tay Canal Basin in the downtown core.

Perth's architectural heritage is best explored on a walking tour. Several houses, business establishments and public buildings are considered the best examples of their kind in tradition and style. Inge-Va and the McMartin House properties are maintained by the Ontario Heritage Foundation. The Perth Museum, named the best small-town museum in 1994 by the Ontario Historical Society, is located in the Matheson House, an 1840 Georgian stone edifice on Gore Street. Perth's architectural style is not static; buildings represent several different decades and styles, including the recent glass pavilion by the Tay Basin, remodelled from the discarded Rideau bus-mall in Ottawa.

Heritage House Museum is located a short distance from Old Slys Locks at Smiths Falls. Completed by Joshua Bates near the site of his mills in 1862, his house stood adjacent to the Brockville & Ottawa Railway. An investment in that railway led to his financial ruin.

14

SMITHS FALLS AND THE SWALE

In the predawn mist, hunters lie low in their makeshift blinds and shallow punts, waiting anxiously for the distinctive flutter of wings that precedes a descending flock of ducks. Deep in the myriad channels of the Smiths Falls Swale, the silence is broken by the wail of a train on the last major line through this small industrial town. The train thunders across the ancient stone CPR bridge over the Rideau Canal, and then the silence returns. A stone's throw from blind or punt rests a small fleet of wooden decoys. Whispers in the wind, then the whistle of wings, and the crack of gunfire rips through the air.

The damp silences and deafening blasts are familiar sounds during the annual duck-hunting season in the Rideau wetlands. In the Smiths Falls Swale, the duck hunt was more than a sporting adventure; it was an annual ritual, a cultural event. The handcrafted decoys and boats were as much a part of the tradition as the hunt itself.

The Smiths Falls Swale, as the broad marshes of the Rideau River above the town are called, has had a significant impact on the town. The swale is an ancient wetland that was broadened by the construction of the Rideau Canal. The Rideau River rapids at Poonamalie, Smiths Falls and Old Slys were tamed by the canal, creating several miles of marshy lands where early residents found good fishing and hunting.

Smiths Falls was slow to develop because of a half-century dispute over the ownership of milling and water-power rights. The water power gave energy to a series of grist, saw and carding mills that formed an industrial centre to the town. The Woods Mill is now home to the Rideau Canal Museum. Foundries played a central role, especially with the development of the huge Frost and Woods Agricultural Implements factory. Smiths Falls was also a strategic hub for railway ventures, including the Brockville & Ottawa Railway (1858), the Southern Ontario routes of the Canadian Pacific Railway (1884), and the Canadian Northern Railway (1913).

The historic bascule railway bridge that still guards the western entrance to the Swale and the nearby Smiths Falls Railway Museum are remnants of the abandoned CN line. To the east, the CPR bridge forms another gateway to the broad lowlands and marshes of the Rideau, from Old Sly's through Edmund's and Kilmarnock Locks to Merrickville. Bounded by the railway lines, the town of Smiths

Harold and Lloyd Nichol on O'Mearas Bay, Big Rideau Lake, standing by Gran D, a 1927 launch built by their great-uncle, Davy Nichol, a famous Smiths Falls boat-builder and decoy carver. Harold maintains the bird-carving tradition in the original workshop.

Falls thrived, and beyond them, the marshes flourished.

One family of boatbuilders and woodcarvers has earned a livelihood and drawn inspiration from the swale and the birds that thrive there. Davy Nichol, who died at the age of ninety in 1949, was attached to the wetlands in work and play. He built wooden skiffs, launches and duck boats for use on the Rideau Canal, and he designed and carved wooden duck decoys for the hunting sorties he so enjoyed. His boats and ducks are considered exquisite examples of an art form and have been collected by the Canadian Museum of Nature and the Canadian Museum of Science and Technology. Two of his boats, *Rideau Passage* and *Gran D*, are favourites at the annual Ottawa International Classic and Antique Boat Show.

The senior Davy Nichol could never have imagined the extent to which his woodworking skills would be celebrated. He passed on his carving skills to his nephew David K. Nichol, who during a forty-year career with Frost and Woods found time to carve every species of North American duck and goose, and whose work is now in the collection of the Museum of Nature. Davy's grandnephew, Harold Nichol, has continued the tradition of carving birds of every kind, to international acclaim. Harold Nichol still lives at the old family home nestled by the canal in Smiths Falls, and the boat shed is remains for storing wood for carving.

A flight of three combined locks was abandoned and a single electric-powered lock installed during a major waterfront redevelopment at Smiths Falls in 1972. The old locks reveal the operating and structural nature of Rideau locks. All but three of the locks on the Rideau still use original or slightly modified hand-operated mechanisms.

The swale and marshes have inspired craftsmanship and excellence, but they now require patience and protection. Only recently have wetlands been given the recognition they deserve as the lifeblood of a river system. Wetlands provide nutrients, absorb floodwaters, form wildlife habitat and sustain a living environment. Formerly considered a wasteland by landowners, an impediment to expansion by developers, and a source of mosquitoes by campers and boaters, they are now understood as an essential element of lake and river health. The Smiths Falls Swale is regarded as one of the most important wetlands in Southern Ontario.

Lieutenant-Colonel John By hated marshes, but he probably did more to create Rideau wetlands than any natural source. His method of building a slackwater canal flooded large sections of land, creating shallow bays and pools where wildlife found habitat and refuge. Like many engineers of the time, By thought that marshes bred disease, and the malaria outbreaks during canal construction increased his fears. No longer inhibited by the threat of malaria, we can appreciate a system of vibrant wetlands extending from Kingston to Ottawa along the Rideau Waterway. This great system includes such major complexes as the Greater Cataraqui Marshes, the River Styx, Murphy's Bay on Lake Opinicon, Newboro Bog, the Big Rideau wetland complex, McLean's Bay, the Tay Marsh, Bacchus Marsh, Smiths Falls Swale, Irish Creek, Merrickville Wildlife Reserve (Federal Migratory Bird Sanctuary), and Cranberry Creek on the Long Reach.

The common loon, lady's slipper orchid, largemouth bass, great blue heron, white-tailed deer, osprey, lake trout, beaver, bluebird, muskrat, many species of duck, and migrating geese are among the diverse species at home in the Rideau Waterway. Flooded lands and marshes are an essential part of the Rideau landscape, and by sustaining wildlife, they continue to provide an important habitat.

The Rideau Canal hosts one of the most important biological research stations in Ontario, operated by Queen's University on Lake Opinicon. The construction of the Rideau Canal inadvertently created an ideal workshop for studies in understanding changes in landscapes and environments over a long period of time. The Queen's University Biological Station was created by Professor Wes Curran, with the research centre opening in 1946 and now encompassing 4,500 acres (1,820 ha) of land managed by Frank Phelan, professor of biology.

Walking the Rideau Trail, a cleared and marked footpath snaking 180 miles (300 km) between Kingston and Ottawa, is the best alternative to boating for investigating the wetlands of the Rideau. The Rideau Trail guide notes cattail marshes, bogs, cedar swamps, and hardwood swamps, with special attention given to Frontenac and Murphy's Point Provincial Parks, the Tay Marsh, the Marlborough Forest, and Stony Swamp Con-

The Rideau Waterway contains some of Ontario's most precious wetlands, some with ancient origins and others created by the building of the Rideau Canal, opened in 1832.

Arthur Briggs-Jude, an award-winning writer and naturalist, stands by a hummingbird haven at his farm, which is known as Blue Bird Acres, and serves as an outdoor education centre on County Road 36 near Westport.

The gentle landscaping of Edmund's Lock

servation Area. There is an observation point over the Tay Marsh at each end, at the Perth Wildlife Reserve and above Beveridges Locks. At the lower lock at Beveridges Locks, take note of the osprey-nest platforms installed on poles provided by Ontario Hydro.

The marshes and wetlands of the Rideau inspired one journalist in 1831 to describe the route under construction as "tedious and doubtful." The drowned lands, water-logged forests and seemingly endless marshes that worried early travellers are now recognized as a valuable and essential part of the character and attraction of the Rideau Canal. Although in Europe the term "canal" can still evoke murky industrial channels, in this part of Canada, "canal" means corridors like the Rideau Canal, a thriving, life-supporting waterway passing through diverse areas of pristine beauty and natural significance.

Merrickville lock station at dawn

15

MERRICKVILLE, BURRITT'S RAPIDS AND THE LONG REACH

The Rideau Canal was a boon to Merrickville. The first mill erected there in 1790 anchored an isolated inland settlement controlled by William Merrick and his family. John By noted in 1830 that the village was flourishing, "not arising from the Workmen employed by Government, but in consequence of the Canal passing through it." The village emerged as one of the most significant industrial centres on the canal.

The Merrickville blockhouse was the largest of four blockhouses erected on the Rideau Canal by Lieutenant-Colonel By. Overlooking the locks, bridge and dam, it is a visible reminder of the original military function of the Rideau Canal and remains a significant landmark on the canal.

By had considered building blockhouses to protect all of the lock stations on the Rideau Canal. Once expenses spiralled out of control, blockhouses were erected only at the entrance locks at Kingston Mills, and at Newboro and Narrows locks to guard the summit of the canal. A citadel planned for Parliament Hill and a blockhouse at Burritt's Rapids never left By's drawing board. Roads connecting Merrickville to the St. Lawrence frontier made the locks and dam there more vulnerable to attack by Americans if an invasion occurred.

The Merrickville blockhouse, designed to serve as a barracks for fifty men, a storage depot for arms and ammunition, and as a defensive bulwark, had first-storey walls made of limestone masonry 4 feet (1.2 m) thick at the base. Gun ports for mounted cannon were located in each stone wall. The thick hewn timber of the second storey had loopholes (openings for small-arms fire) on all four sides and through the base of the overhang to enable defenders to fire at any enemy reaching the walls. A wooden ramp over a dry moat, like a drawbridge to a medieval fortress, provided access to an opening in the second floor facing the lock.

Never attacked, the blockhouse did serve military purposes on two occasions. When British troops were dispersed to points in Upper Canada during the Rebellion of 1837–38, Merrickville served as a temporary barracks for the 34th Regiment while they were en route to Amherstburg. The Oregon Crisis of 1846 (when American expansionists cried "fifty-four forty or fight" regarding the western boundary between Canada and the

United States, ultimately set at the 49th parallel) turned the blockhouse into a planned headquarters for the defence of the Rideau in case of war, and a fall-back position should Americans gain control on the St. Lawrence. Regular troops, however, did not garrison the building.

Like the other blockhouses, the Merrickville blockhouse was used as a lockmaster's home. Restored in the early 1960s as a result of the growing interest in heritage structures, today the blockhouse serves as a popular local museum and is at the centre of a renewal of Merrickville that has been taking place over the past two decades. On the island the ruins of an industrial complex are open to the public, and on the north bank several industrial buildings survive, including the existing Alloy Foundry Works, the oldest continuously operating iron foundry in the province. The commercial centre on the south bank has been revived as a significant centre for heritage tourism. Close enough to Ottawa for an afternoon outing, but far enough away to retain its rural charm and village atmosphere, Merrickville is now a place of craft shops, antique stores, art galleries, bookstores, fine restaurants and some of the best bed and breakfast inns in the valley. The blockhouse is only one of many of the architectural gems that grace the village and its outlying areas.

The nearby village of Burritt's Rapids is almost completely surrounded by the Rideau Waterway. The village centre lies between the river to the north and the natural snie (a side channel in a stream) that formed the canal channel to the south, creating an island atmosphere for most of its tiny population. Both river roads leading to the village from Merrickville were important early thoroughfares and remain significant for their rural charm and architectural heritage.

Travellers driving the river roads from Merrickville are enchanted by the legacy left by Rideau stonemasons. On the north side the route passes a number of grand two-storey residences, while the southern route has several storey-and-a-half stone houses. In their symmetrical five-bay facades and gracious classical detail, the buildings celebrate in stone the elements of proportion and simplicity in design that characterize Georgian architecture in Ontario and especially the Rideau corridor. At Upper Nicholson's Locks and the wooden swing-bridge near the ghost town of Andrewsville, it is a worthwhile stroll up the canal bank to Lower Nicholson's Locks. Of special interest is the character of the brick house on the east bank, with its elliptical fan-lighted doorway facing river and road. The setting of pasture, trees and canal is magical.

About twenty families were living in the immediate area of Burritt's Rapids when the canal was completed. On the north side of the riverbank, Christ Church (1831), the stone Burritt House, and a couple of country inns and taverns were part of the original village

The McCrae House near Merrickville is one of the earliest stone houses in Montague Township, dating from the early 1820s, before stonemasons from the canal left their imprint on the landscape. With or without the later addition of the central gable peak, it is typical of a vernacular style of architecture on the Rideau.

A stone house with a Regency flavour in Merrickville, once the home of Aaron Merrick, a prominent merchant-miller-developer, and later, Harry Falconer McLean, a construction tycoon responsible for railway and hydroelectric development in the north.

Intricate polychromatic brick design (red and yellow bricks laid in Flemish bond style, alternately lengthwise and crosswise in every row) fashions this and several homes in the Burritt's Rapids, Merrickville and Easton's Corners areas.

Rideau symmetry and simplicity near Burritt's Rapids. The Campbell House, built in 1840, was likely built by stonemasons hired to build the Rideau Canal.

The William Merrick House, overlooking his former mill-site, is a Georgian building overlaid with later Victorian ornamentation. The Merrick family once owned all the land where Merrickville now thrives, but they sold off properties in the 1850s and 1860s when Merrickville's industrial core was booming.

centre. The canal drew settlers onto the "island," toward the swing bridge over the canal. The lock station itself is downstream, somewhat removed from the village. Overshadowed by the industrial might of Merrickville upriver, Burritt's Rapids nevertheless had its own saw, grist and woollen mills and became an agricultural service centre.

Burritt's Rapids has two of the Rideau's most picturesque village churches. Inside and out, the simple rectangular buildings reflect an interest in the Gothic Revival style of architecture, which included pointed or arched windows and door openings. The earliest, Christ Church, built for the Church of England and Ireland congregation formed in 1822, was finished the year before the completion of the Rideau Canal. Accompanying Lieutenant-Colonel By from Kingston to Ottawa in May 1832, a surprised Edward John Barker, editor of the *British Whig*, remarked, "A rather unusual sight here presents itself – a handsome Episcopal Church upon a rising ground, betokeing a state of society not altogether expected."

The most distinctive elements of Christ Church are its decorative tower with quoins, crenellations and pinnacles, and its curved gallery face supported on four turned Tuscan columns. In a spectacular display of good intentions and short-sighted indifference, the

Dawn at the swing bridge over the canal at Burritt's Rapids.

building was covered in vinyl siding in 1992, covering up one hundred and sixty years' worth of wood siding.

The Wesley Methodist Church was built overlooking the banks of the Rideau Canal at Burritt's Rapids in 1855. One can imagine the faithful strolling along the shoreline in their Sunday finest after a summer service. Methodism had taken root in Ontario from the arrival of the United Empire Loyalists and was reinforced by later settlement. The needs of the earliest settlers were served by circuit-riders who would preach in the homes of adherents. Theirs was a religion of evangelical passion, where the hand of God was seen in everyday experience. The congregation joined the United Church in the Union of 1925, but since 1974, it has been silent. The stalwart Merrickville United Church, planted solidly across the road from the blockhouse, absorbed at least part of the congregation. However, a piece of the village fabric and vitality was lost with its closing. One church has lost its interior, the other, its exterior.

Religion was a major part of the social world of Ontario in the nineteenth century. It helped form a sense of order, familiarity and tradition for arriving immigrants, and sustained a world view that characterized the sense of place and morality in the community.

The wake from Murray and Sarah Gould's historic 1927 Chris-Craft runabout, Warpath, *as it glides over the Long Reach, where strips of cottages and homes cling to the riverbank.*

Owing to the largely Irish-Protestant nature of settlement in the area between 1820 and 1855, and Irish-Catholic settlement resulting from the construction of the canal and the Irish famine in the mid-1840s, a tension existed that gave rise to the Loyal Orange Lodge. Added to this mix were what historian Glenn Lockwood has identified as earlier settlers of American origin being confronted by settlers of British origin among the immigrants moving into the Rideau corridor; all these differences affected local politics, temperance and moral issues. Tensions along the system almost boiled over during the 1830s. The Fenian crises in 1866 and 1870 gave rise to anti-Catholic organizations such as the Dark Lantern Association in Kemptville and Merrickville, and revived the more established Orange Lodge (one branch is still active in Burritt's Rapids).

Beyond Burritt's Rapids lies the Long Reach, a stretch of navigable waterway about 26 miles (45 km) to the next locks at Long Island. Beckett's Landing Bridge is named after an early settler, Thomas A. Beckett, who arrived in the 1830s and was a hotel keeper, wool carder, brewer and bridgemaster. When the first swing bridge at the landing was constructed in 1858, Thomas Beckett was appointed the tender, and there was still a Beckett manning the bridge fifty years later.

Kemptville Creek, the third-largest tributary of the Rideau River, enters just downstream of Beckett's Landing. Sir James Kempt, administrator of the Government of Canada from 1828 to 1830 and the author of the report that supported Lieutenant-Colonel By's plans for locks to handle steamboat traffic on the Rideau Canal, gave his name to the village and a creek that had no lock itself. Like Elgin to the south, Kemptville has developed slightly removed from the canal, but also as a part of it. Steamers familiar with the limited depth of the Rideau Canal used to make their way up the creek to Clothier's mills. Because of the patronage of a prominent Ontario premier, the town is the site of the Kemptville College of Agricultural Technology, begun in 1917, and the G. Howard Ferguson Forest Station, named in his honour in 1945. Nearby is Rideau River Provincial Park and the Baxter Creek and W.A. Taylor Conservation Areas.

Below Kars, the shoreline of the Rideau River takes on an increasingly altered character. Strips of cottages, many now transformed into permanent homes, hug the riverbanks. Large farms were gradually displaced by encroaching subdivisions as commuters were attracted to the river environment close to a rapidly expanding Ottawa. Most buildings date from the 1960s and 1970s, but several of the more conspicuously grand edifices were built in the 1980s. At the Long Island lock station, one of Lieutenant-Colonel By's spectacular keywork stone arch dams graces the landscape. The Long Reach acts as a transition zone, buffering the rural character of the Rideau River from the encroaching thrusts of suburbia.

The home of Moss Kent Dickinson is overshadowed by his 1860 stone grist mill, now known as Watson's Mill, an operating mill-museum managed by the Rideau Valley Conservation Authority, which uses the historic house as its headquarters. Dickinson modelled the frame house, built in 1867, after Abraham Lincoln's house in Springfield, Illinois.

16

KING OF THE RIDEAU

Moss Kent Dickinson was a businessman who forged new links during the transition of the Rideau Canal from military to commercial purpose, and he campaigned all his life for a living, essential waterway through the heart of Eastern Ontario. He was born in Canada's first canal age in the 1820s and died toward the end of the second in the 1890s. As the founder of Manotick, he envisioned a new community based on the availability of water power on the Rideau River; and through the operation of his canal boats, and later, his concern for water resources, he kept issues relating to the Rideau Canal on the agenda of the nation.

The Rideau Canal was built as a military system to protect against the Americans by providing an inland transportation alternative to the St. Lawrence River, which was so vulnerable to attack from the south. Dickinson had a hand in turning the canal into a corridor to the United States. Born in Lewis County in upper New York State in 1822, Moss Dickinson followed his father, Barnabus, who was a founder of Dickinson's Landing on the St. Lawrence, into the forwarding trade. Barnabus Dickinson died in the cholera epidemic of 1832, but Moss was educated in the trade by his father's former business associates and relations. By 1844, Moss Dickinson was forwarding agricultural produce in the Montréal–Ottawa–Kingston triangle. His outlets to American markets were through both the Richelieu and Chambly Canals and the Oswego Canal, and by 1865 his Ottawa and Rideau Transportation Line operated eleven steamers, fifty-five barges and several tugboats.

Forwarding, the art of transporting and transhipping goods on the waterway, was a colourful enterprise. Side-wheel and propellor steamers towed wooden barges among other bateau and Durham boats traversing the system. Unlike the Erie Canal, which had towpaths, low bridges, and rapidly developing urban centres, the Rideau was a challenge to boat captains. They had to be ever wary of the river and lake beyond the channel, and were completely dependent upon their own navigational skills; there were no teamsters on convenient paths to catch a line.

Where on the Erie there emerged a sort of folklore associated with the interaction between canal users and the public, on the Rideau, stories of travel on the canal were closely held by the crews on board and the lockmen at isolated stations between Kingston and Ottawa. In Ottawa, the crews mixed with

Sunset over the Rideau near Manotick

the swaggering and boisterous logging and sawmill gangs, and in Kingston, they joined up with the Great Lakes mariners. Unfortunately, few stories of the history of forwarding on the Rideau survive.

A partnership between Joseph Merrill Currier (who in 1867 built 24 Sussex Drive, the Prime Minister's residence in Ottawa) and Moss Kent Dickinson led to the purchase in 1858 of a mill seat at Long Island in the Rideau River. They erected a grist mill there in 1860. Only a month after Currier married Ann Crosby in 1861, she was killed while touring the mill when her dress was caught up in the machinery and she was hurled against a pillar. This shocking event caused Currier to lose interest in the mill, which to this day is said to be haunted by her ghost.

The Long Island milling enterprises were solely owned by Moss Dickinson after 1863, and he developed the emerging Manotick village site as a single-industry town around M.K. Dickinson's General Trading and Manufacturing Depot and Farmer's Exchange. The stone grist mill; wood-framed sawmill; shingle mill; carding mill; bung, plug and spile factory (manufacturing barrel plugs and bottle caps); and cooper's and carpenter's shops formed the centre of a new community.

The King of the Rideau served as mayor of Ottawa from 1864 to 1866, living across from Currier in the present residence of the South African High Commission, and he sold his interest in the forwarding empire in 1869 to concentrate fully on the Manotick enterprise. Four hundred people were living in Manotick by 1879. When elected to Parliament in 1882, Dickinson championed canal interests, including the building of the second Tay Canal to Perth, which was in part designed to improve water flow on the Rideau system.

The surviving original stone mill (Watson's Mill) and house now form a focal point in old Manotick known as Dickinson's Square. The site is maintained by the Rideau Valley Conservation Authority as a functioning mill-museum and a headquarters for the authority. The vitality of the square and surrounding neighbourhood are signs of the power of the Rideau to entice new patterns of settlement, first in 1860, and then after the Second World War, attracting residential development associated not only with the growth of Ottawa, but also with an appreciation of the Rideau Valley as a place to live and seek recreation.

Few individuals have had such a lasting effect on the viability of the Rideau Canal as Moss Kent Dickinson. Like Thomas McKay of Ottawa, who created the community of New Edinburgh at Rideau Falls, Dickinson was responsible for Manotick, and he forged a commercial and industrial purpose for the canal even after the demand for forwarding had declined. The Rideau Canal remained a vital link between regions and nations because of his efforts.

Crossing the Rideau River by way of Green Island, the historic Minto Bridges, dating from 1900, were part of a ceremonial route between the governor-general's house at Rideau Hall and the Parliament buildings and formed a gateway to New Edinburgh.

17

THROUGH THE HEART OF THE NATION'S CAPITAL

High above Nepean Point, with a vista over the Ottawa River and the entrance to the Rideau Canal, stands a statue of Samuel de Champlain, the French explorer who, during a trip up the river in 1615, so the story goes, gave the name Rideau to the sheet of water pouring over the escarpment like a curtain. It was two hundred and eleven years later at that site, which would become Bytown, later Ottawa, and Canada's national capital, that Lieutenant-Colonel John By began planning the means by which the Rideau River could be tamed into a navigable waterway.

It is hard to imagine what By thought in 1826 when he looked at the limestone escarpment that formed what would be Parliament Hill and Nepean Point. It is alleged that Lord Dalhousie sought to purchase lands at the more gentle incline near the Chaudiere Falls, but was rebuffed by the extravagant demands of landowners LeBreton and Rankin. The contract was let to Thomas McKay to build a flight of locks in a convenient but imposing entrance valley. Lieutenant-Colonel By erected his home on the east side of the entrance on the site of Major's Hill Park, and envisaged a citadel, later only a series of military barracks, on Parliament Hill on the opposite side. The Ottawa River entrance was flanked by the Royal Engineer's office and the Ordnance warehouse; the warehouse still stands as Ottawa's oldest building, and houses both the Bytown Museum and the archives of the Historical Society of Ottawa.

Soon after McKay had gouged out the cavity for the first two locks, he was informed by Lieutenant-Colonel By that the canal must be made be wider than was formerly specified. By had been successful at convincing military authorities to opt for locks that would permit the passing of steamships, making the Rideau the first steamboat canal in North America. McKay started anew, and the final product was the greatest achievement in masonry lock building on the canal, the flight of eight locks at Ottawa.

Above Ottawa Locks the first Sapper's bridge connected Lower Town with Upper Town, both communities being created by the impact of canal construction. Queen Victoria announced the site of Bytown as the new capital of Canada in 1858, and Parliament buildings constructed in the Gothic style were completed by the early 1860s. The present east and west blocks are original, but the centre block and tower were constructed after the fire of 1916. Architectural historian Harold Kalman claims that these Victorian buildings were not mere imitations of European models, but rather the best of their kind in the world, with high walls, steep roofs, and a sense of roughly textured massiveness that helped to create a national style.

The grounds were carefully and generously landscaped, an influence that eventually crept down the side of Parliament Hill to the locks, and up along the east side to Major's Hill Park and overlooking the locks where the Château Laurier rose between 1911 and 1913. It too was distinctively Canadian, in the grand tradition of railway hotels in Canada. The construction of the Rideau Canal influenced the location of early public buildings such as the demolished post office and city hall (the new city hall now sits on an island in the middle of the Rideau River just above the falls), Confederation Square and the War Memorial, Union Railway Station and, more recently, the National Arts Centre. The new National Art Gallery on Nepean Point and the Museum of Civilization across the Ottawa River in Hull are the latest shining additions to one of Canada's most significant cultural landscapes.

Ottawa is the second-coldest capital city in the world. Northwest winds whip down the Ottawa Valley like an express train, sending pedestrians scurrying. Some walk gingerly, like penguins, afraid to find an icy patch under a layer of snow that will send them on a skid or worse. Others head for the ice on the canal, strap on skates, and glide to work on the longest skating-rink in the world.

Ottawa is home to a skating rink that stretches along the Rideau Canal from Hartwell's Locks, through the expanse of Dow's Lake, all the way to the Ottawa Locks sheltered between the shoulders of Parliament Hill and the Château Laurier. The rink started as a patch of ice 295 yards (270 m) long cleared by the National Capital Commission in 1970 and is now approximately 4 1/2 miles (6 km) long, encompassing a surface of 1,794,000 square yards (1,500,000 m^2). In spite of wind and snow, many Ottawa residents skate to work in late December, January, February and early March. Others come to the canal for leisurely weekend or evening skates. The city comes alive for three weekends of celebration during Ottawa's famous Winterlude carnival in February.

Skating, snowshoeing, skiing and tobaganing parties have long been a feature of Ottawa's winter season. When the National Capital Commission in co-operation with the Rideau Canal and Parks Canada first opened the skating rink, the city was overwhelmed by the success. On sunny weekends when thousands take to their skates the canal is an explosion of colour; where early skaters were once bundled in blue, brown and grey (and the occasional colourful Hudson's Bay Company parka), now all the colours of the rainbow flash against the dazzling white of ice and

A flight of eight Ottawa Locks at the entrance valley. The stone Commissariat building was constructed in 1827 as a warehouse for military and canal supplies. The oldest building in the city, it houses the Bytown Museum of the Historical Society of Ottawa.

An Ottawa winter: a riot of colourful skaters on the longest skating-rink in the world.

snow and sky. Looking north from the middle of the ice to the Château Laurier as skaters sweep to the end of the rink on a Winterlude weekend is like viewing a kaleidoscope of colours being swept up into a fairytale castle.

Early on, skating on the Rideau was a favoured pastime of governor-generals and their guests. In 1872, when Lord Dufferin arrived in Ottawa to take up his duties at Rideau Hall, he complained about "the solitude, desolation and incompleteness of the capital." In order to liven up their "dull and lonely" life in the winter, the Dufferins promoted amateur theatricals and winter sports. They built a private rink and a toboggan slide on the grounds, and their successors, the Marquis of Lorne and the Marquis of Lansdowne, Lord Stanley, the Earl of Aberdeen, as well as the Earl of Minto, continued the tradition of skating parties. Festive skaters at Rideau Hall wore white blanket-cloth coats, knickerbockers, purple stockings, red sashes and knitted toques, and glided around a rink festooned with coloured fairy lamps and Japanese lanterns.

The Earl of Minto founded the Minto Skating Club, which has been home to such figure-skating champions as Barbara Ann Scott and Elizabeth Manley. One early commentator wrote, "There are not many men in Ottawa who skate sufficiently well to show Lady Minto off to advantage." Lord and Lady Minto were in attendance when the Ottawa Silver Seven successfully defended the Stanley Cup, defeating the Dawson City Klondikers at the Aberdeen Pavilion next to the Rideau Canal in 1905. Lord Stanley donated the cup in 1892 in honour of the sport of ice hockey, which found its Canadian origins at the other end of the canal in Kingston when the British garrison experimented with shinny in the 1850s. This enthusiasm for skating and other winter sports in Ottawa never diminished and was an impetus for the creation of the Rideau Canal rink in 1970. Many people from warmer climes come to Ottawa in the winter to participate in this distinctly Canadian attraction. Ottawa may be one of the coldest capitals in winter, but its skating tradition inspires a sense of warmth and camaraderie that enlivens an ice-bound canal in the middle of a bustling city.

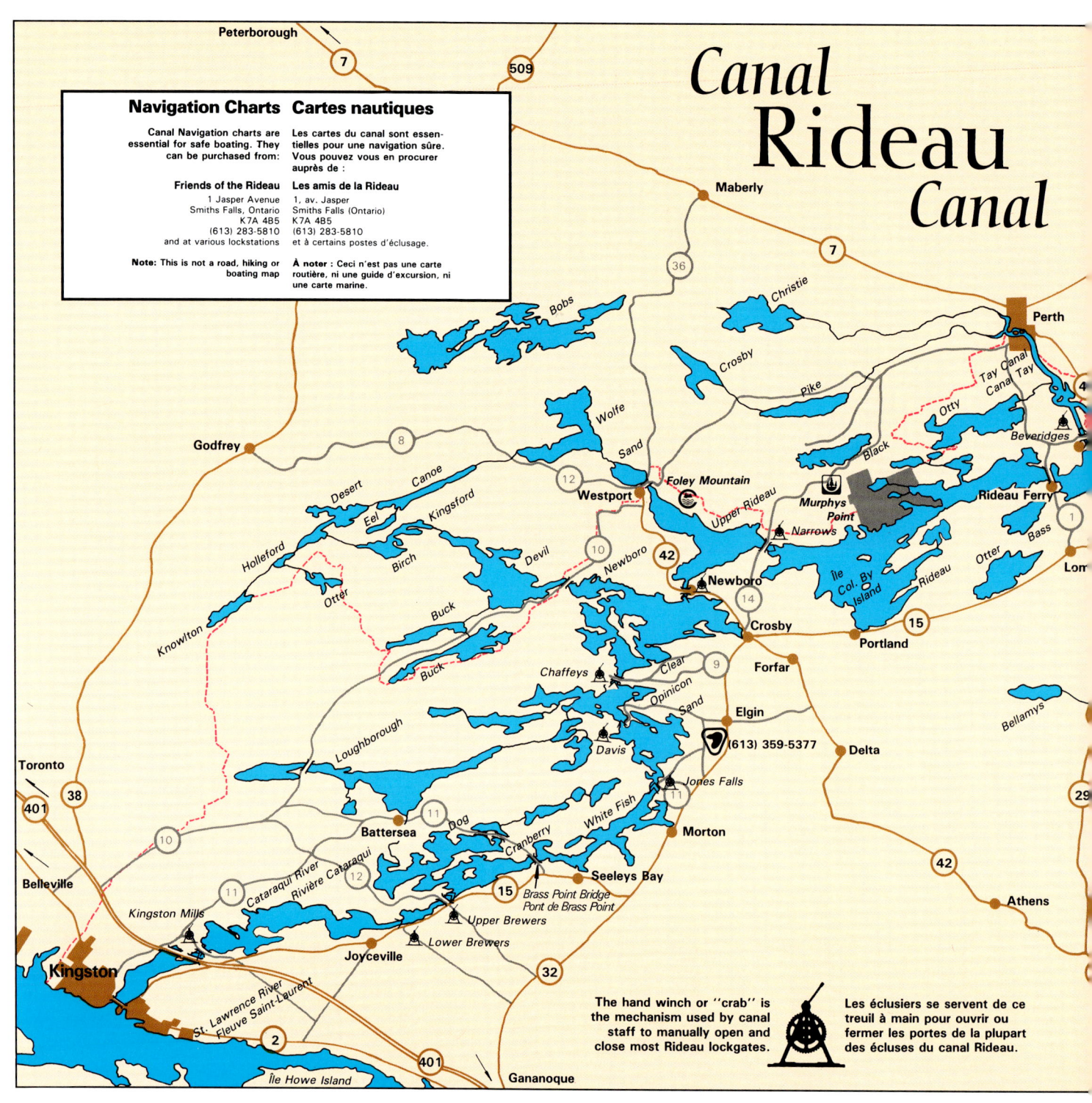

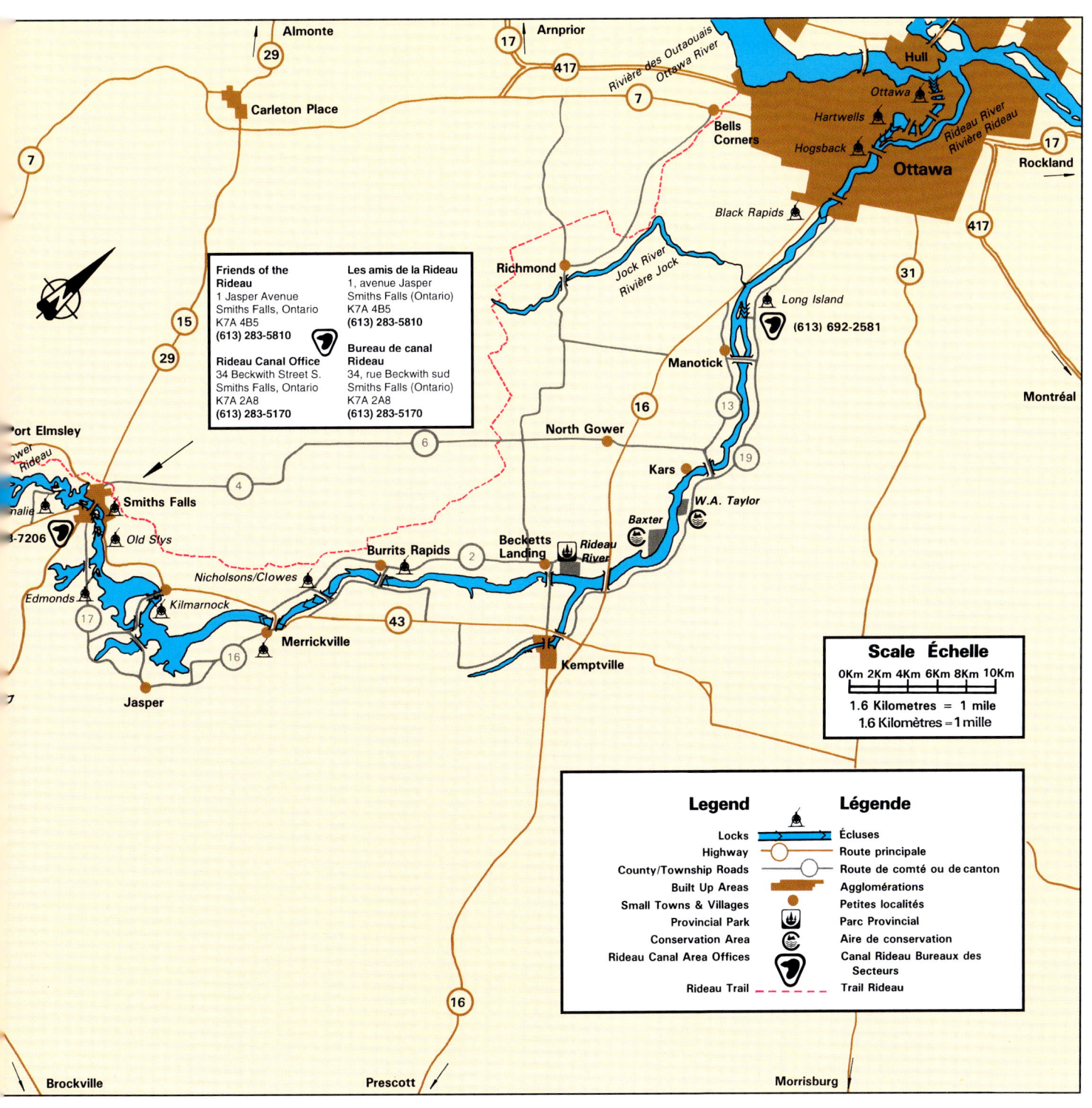

A NOTE ON SOURCES

The depth of original materials on the Rideau Canal, cartographic, iconographic, photographic and documentary, is outstanding. Any search for Rideau Canal material begins at the National Archives of Canada in record group, manuscript group, cartographic and photographic archive divisions. These sources are too numerous to mention here, but have been extensively mined by Parks Canada since 1972, with results of research published in limited editions in their Rideau Canal Preliminary Site Studies Series, Manuscript Report Series, and Microfiche Report Series. The latter two are available at Parks Canada regional office libraries, provincial and territorial archive libraries, and the Natural Resources Library, U.S. Department of the Interior, Washington, D.C., and the National Library of Canada, Ottawa. A bibliography of these sources has been compiled by Larry Turner as *Rideau Canal Bibliography 1972–1992* (Smiths Falls: Friends of the Rideau, 1992).

Original Rideau Canal material is also stored at the Archives of Ontario, Toronto; Royal Ontario Museum, Toronto; Queen's University Archives, Kingston; and various historical society and museum collections along the Rideau corridor. See also collections of primary and secondary source material at Parks Canada Ontario Region Office, Cornwall, and Rideau Canal Office, Smiths Falls.

SELECT BIBLIOGRAPHY

Barker, Edward John. *Observations on the Rideau Canal.* Kingston: Office of the British Whig, 1834.

Carroll, Catherine L. *King of the Rideau: A Novel Based on the Life of Moss Kent Dickinson.* Manotick: Rideau Valley Conservation Authority, 1974.

Douglas, Alec, and Larry Turner eds. *On a Sunday Afternoon: Classic Boats on the Rideau Canal.* Erin: Boston Mills Press, 1989.

Elliott, Bruce S. *The City Beyond: A History of Nepean, Birthplace of Canada's Capital 1792–1990.* Corporation of the City of Nepean, 1991.

Fleming, Clint. *When the Fish are Rising: Tales of the Rideau Lakes.* New York: Duell, Sloan and Pearce, 1947.

Fleming, Laurel. *Hearth and Heritage: History of the Chaffey's Lock and Area 1800–1980.* Kingston: Brown & Martin, 1981.

Fryer, Mary Beacock and Adrian G. Ten Cate, *The Rideau: A Pictorial History of the Waterway.* Brockville: Besancourt, 1981.

George, Victor A. "The Rideau Corridor: The Effect of a Canal System on a Frontier Region, 1832–1898." M.A. Thesis, Queen's University, 1972.

Gordanier, Deborah A. *Rideau Heritage.* Inverary: Rideau Prints, 1982.

Gwyn, Sandra. *The Private Capital: Ambition and Love in the Age of Macdonald and Laurier.* Toronto: McClelland and Stewart, 1984.

Kalman, Harold. *A History of Canadian Architecture.* Toronto: Oxford University Press, 1994.

Kennedy, James R. *South Elmsley in the Making 1783–1983.* Corporation of the Township of South Elmsley, 1984.

Legget, Robert. *John By: Builder of the Rideau Canal, Founder of Ottawa.* Ottawa: Historical Society of Ottawa, 1982.

Legget, Robert. *Rideau Waterway.* Toronto: University of Toronto Press, 1955.

Lockwood, Glenn J. *Montague: A Social History of an Irish Ontario Township 1783–1980.* Corporation of the Township of Montague, 1980.

Lockwood, Glenn, J. *Smiths Falls: A Social History of the Men and Women in a Rideau Canal Community, 1794–1994.* Corporation of the Town of Smiths Falls, 1994.

Mactaggart, John. *Three Years in Canada: An Account of the Actual State of the Country in 1826-7-8*. London: Henry Colburn, 1829, 2 Vol.

Osborne, Brian S. and Donald Swainson. *Kingston: Building on the Past*. Westport: Butternut Press, 1988.

Moore, D. Jane. *Rideau Passages*. Cloyne: Mapleware Publishing, 1982.

Passfield, Robert W. *Building the Rideau Canal: A Pictorial History*. Toronto: Fitzhenry and Whiteside in association with Parks Canada, 1982.

Peck, Mary E. *From War to Winterlude: 150 Years on the Rideau Canal*. Ottawa: Public Archives of Canada, 1982.

Raudzens, George. *The British Ordnance Department and Canada's Canals 1815–1855*. Waterloo: Sir Wilfrid Laurier University Press, 1979.

Reid, Richard M. *The Upper Ottawa Valley to 1855*. Ottawa: Carleton University Press for the Champlain Society, 1990.

Sneyd, Robert B. "The Role of the Rideau Waterway, 1826–56." M.A. Thesis, University of Toronto, 1965.

Taylor, John H. *Ottawa: An Illustrated History*. Toronto: Lorimer, 1986.

Turner, Larry. *Merrickville: Jewel on the Rideau: A History and Guide*. Ottawa: Petherwin Heritage, 1995.

Turner, Larry with John J. Stewart, *Perth: Tradition and Style in Eastern Ontario*. Toronto: Natural Heritage/ Natural History Inc., 1992.

Walker, Harry and Olive. *Carlton Saga*. Ottawa: Carleton County Council, 1968.

Wells, Kenneth McNeill. *Cruising the Rideau Waterway*. Toronto: McClelland and Stewart, 1965.